<u>Revi</u>

MW01223623

An Amazing and Entert
with tons of information t
photographs are worth the price alone. This is not a rehash, it is filled with information that you won't have been aware of. There is lots to learn in this great book. I recommend this as the perfect gift book for friends and family." – *Ricki Dunn*

Fraser's "Early Entertainment" Shows How We Got Here From There: Others have given this book five stars, and I'm inclined to as well. It contains a wealth of information about a nearly forgotten part of our nation's history. As a history Teacher, I think it is vital to give students an appreciation for the settings in which important events have taken place. Entertainment is an important backdrop to our country's phenomenal progress. Anyone who wishes to truly understand the rich history of the United States of America should have a copy of this amazing chronology. Mr. Fraser does a wonderful job of entertaining us as he fills us in on how Americans spent much of their leisure time back when the U.S.A. was still a young nation, struggling to find her place in the world. Quite simply, you owe it to yourself to read Fraser's lively account of a time before entertainment could be turned on and off with an electronic switch. Brilliant in conception and presentation! – *Charles Stansfield*

A book of historic musical significance, filled with rare pictures!!! This articulately written history book of early music is comprehensive, insightful and entertaining. I love all of the rare and historic photographs that Prof Douglas Fraser chose to include. He has literally put a wealth of knowledge under my "Kindle" fingertips...for instant acess whenever and where ever. (Old timey info using Flash Gordon technology...)I give this book FIVE stars and most highly recommend it to players and musicologists and truth seekers everywhere! – *Mark E. Josephs*

This book is filled with secrets, surprises, and delights.

You will be introduced to, and become quite intimate with, the creation of everything that makes up entertainment and the activities that brought smiles to the faces of North America. Covering the roots of jazz, vaudeville, burlesque, big bands, silent movies, ragtime, television, bare-knuckle prize fights, minstrel shows, circus and carnivals, bebop, medicine shows, jug bands, bicycles, musicians' drugs, radio, Model Ts, paddlewheelers, roller-skates, the blues, barnstorming, gramophones, dancing, barbershop quartets, stage microphones, Tin Pan Alley, washboard bands, swing, wild west shows and more. Lots of photographs and insight to subjects that you thought you knew about.

Douglas Edward Fraser is a musicologist with a lifetime of knowledge. He includes many personal and family stories that have been chronicled from the experiences of three generations of professional entertainers. This is a book like no other, and it has been written to entertain and enlighten the readers that enjoy the Old West, Victorian, Edwardian and jazz eras.

Early Entertainment

The Evolution of Show Business

1840 to 1940

"From the days of bare-knuckled prize fighters, smoky backwater saloons, and Barbershop Quartets"

Douglas Edward Fraser

Early Entertainment
The Evolution of Show Business
1840 to 1940
"From the days of bare-knuckled prize fighters, smoky
backwater saloons, and Barbershop Quartets"

ISBN: 1508976945
ISBN-13: 978-1508976943

DEDICATION

This book is dedicated to my wife Jennifer Nelson, whom I love.
This is also dedicated with love to my two wonderful daughters,
Jaime Elizabeth Fraser and Nicole Jane Fraser.

CONTENTS

ACKNOWLEDGMENTS

This is being created in response to all the requests that I have received throughout the years from audiences members who have seen my live performances: requests to put some of it into a book. I have played the songs and told the stories, and now, in depth, I give you the history.

And a most wonderful history it is.

PREAMBLE

This goes out to my father.

My acknowledgement here is to the years of training that my father gave me which infused an interest in this one hundred year era. He taught me to sing and appreciate the music, style and attitudes of our artistic pioneers.

My father's background allowed me to meet many of the interesting creators in show business. Dad had officially retired from the professional stage before I was born: he then combined his circus and stage talents and became a daredevil commercial artist. He advertised "If you need something painted that provides such difficulty, as to be life threatening; having been turned down by all others; bring your money to me." As the years went by, he lost three helpers on these reckless jobs, men who had fallen to their deaths. After these dreadful accidents, he continued on as a commercial sign painter and designer. Even then having his name in the industry brought a connection between his artistic talent and the entertainment world.

My father created logos and painted all of "Evel Knievel's" Triumph motorcycles and helmets in the mid 1960s. Bobby Knievel gave me one of his Bell helmets; I was 14 ½ years old and had just received my first motorcycle. Wanting to show-off to my friends that I knew Evel Knievel, I asked if he would pull one of his bikes out of the truck and go riding with me while dad finished painting the bike for his next big jump. He said, "I never ride on the street, it's too dangerous". I said, "What?!" and, after that, looked a bit let down. Next thing I knew, he pulled up on his jump bike and off we went. I said, "My friends from school hang out at the A&W Drive-in, want to go there?" We cruised the A&W Drive-in, his motorcycle and the way he could ride it, unmistakably said, "Evel Knievel" and there was not one person at the packed drive-in that didn't recognize him. He wheelied all the way around the drive-in and skidded to a stop sideways, stepped off and ordered us both a root beer. Everyone cheered and they stepped out of their cars to applaud. My popularity soared.

One of the other people that my father regularly designed backdrops, posters, and billboards for was the hypnotist "Reveen". Peter Reveen came to my dad with projects that "Would have to be paid for after the next show". My father was always understanding and generous, and knew the ups and downs of show business all too well. He was happy to help, as he did with many other performers as well.

He and my mother owned some restaurants in the Los Angeles area when I was very young. Starving actors would come in and dad would feed them every day. They would sign for their meals with the understanding that if they got a gig, or ever saw some level of success, they were to come in and pay off their tab. Apparently, my dad was famous for feeding actors who were down-and-out. Some would use the money that would have bought them a small sandwich elsewhere to ride the bus, or pay for gas, to arrive at my dad's restaurant where they would eat like kings. Dad always put an extra scoop of mashed potatoes on their plates to help fill them up. Many of those who ate at my dad's, and a few who actually became big stars, would return to pay off all the outstanding tabs, and shower my parents with thank-you gifts. Some of the actors would pilfer small props from the movie sets and leave those as payment, while still signing for their meals. I was too young to realize how interesting a copy of the list of those indebted would be today. But I knew that occasionally my father would tear up the list and start anew.

As a child and a young boy growing up I felt that my father was unlike anyone else.

My father loved the sense of touring; the feeling that he got while in show business. He was a free spirit, and arriving in a new town made him feel refreshed and excited. Hence, every year or so, he would sell or give our house away (he did that twice) with the rules that we were only allowed to take what we could carry (including suitcases). We would leave all other possessions, furniture, collections, motorcycles, cars, records, clothes, sporting equipment, everything else and head out. All these things were to be bought new once we arrived at our new house, which several times he had purchased over the phone. These were houses that did not always stand up to the description given. It didn't matter, he always arrived delighted. "A bit of a fixer-upper", my mother might say, although she never made a negative comment, never complained, and never said no to him over anything. Well only once…

My father loved animals and it was common for us to have dogs, fish, parrots, monkeys and crocodiles at the same time. I remember the day my father came home with a Himalayan sun bear. My mother put her foot down for the first time saying that it was not welcome and had to go back. My dad just turned around and took it out the door. As he passed me he whispered, "It was a pretty good run".

I grew up at a time when children could leave the house in the morning and ride their bike all day. Sometimes I cycled right across the city, or really anywhere as long as I still returned by dinner time. Parents didn't worry back then. When I was about twenty I went to visit my parents. They weren't home but the door was unlocked.

When my dad came home I said, "Did you know that you left the house unlocked?" He said, "Yeah, what if someone came walking up our street and needed a drink of water?" (It was the carefree way he thought). I said, "Ever think of just leaving a glass by the hose?"

Then I said, "Why do you think they put locks on doors"? He responded by saying, "They are to be used by people who can't make friends."

Both my parents are gone now and I miss them dearly. They shaped my wit, my outlook, and my sense of adventure. This book in itself is an adventure that I hope you enjoy.
D.E.F.

INTRODUCTION

Today with social media everyone records their daily thoughts, achievements, and depressions on Facebook and Twitter. Who knows what the next form of public diary will be? The job of historian one hundred years from now will be embarrassingly easy. It will certainly be nothing like the challenge of uncovering events from the nineteenth century and early 20th century.

Musical history, not unlike history in general, is a spirited soul with multiple personalities. The areas of discovery are immense and musicologists tend to condense their focus to certain disciplined categories such as "notable early jazz performers". These historians will know names and information on the artist's early childhood. They are able to list acquaintances, adjudicate their quality of performance, and describe the artist's typical breakfast selections. I am personally thankful for colleagues who maintain this focus and acquire the information we can all turn to for answers. My own curiosity has always been the broader picture.

Many of the facts surrounding historical events and their authors were not chronicled in the 19th and early 20th century. Much of the information was verbally shared and shared again, allowing for embellishment and the loss of details. Historians remain divided on some topics, with groups leaning towards one theory, while others lay claim to yet another: each equally plausible. History is a cruel bedfellow.

The reader of historical events may come across holes in the net, subjects deemed unworthy, or contradictions concerning the outcome of events. Human research can have its flaws. Occasionally, misrepresentation and distortion of historical accounts can be motivated by envy, ill will, favour, flattery, misreading, or misinterpretation. All history is not history. We, who are looked upon to provide the facts, stand on our honour to do our best. An author has the responsibility to let the reader know when something is not stamped in stone. But sometimes, the appearance of rock is misleading and it crumbles to be swept to the curb and replaced by a new more creditable stone.

This book is intended to gently walk the reader through some of the events, stories, and facts that inspired and broke ground for the entertainment that we enjoy today. I will talk about North American music and show business in general. Occasionally, I veer from the subject to inject a tidbit of knowledge that I personally find thought-provoking. Stay with me, as, before you know it, we will be right back on course.

In North America we have created and developed a new music: styles that would not have existed without a unique combination of cultural contributions. When I say we, I speak of the people of the United States and Canada, and all the elements of chance that are forged together when something is invented, developed, or conceived.

If you live in North America, this is your story.

CHAPTER ONE: SLAVERY IN THE AMERICAS

It is awkward to start a book about entertainment with the subject of slavery, but this is where the story of our musical heritage begins. The Black people brought over from the African continent were the motivators in the creation of the new music that would define North America's musical contribution. The African slave that came to North America had a very different musical background from the Europeans, who also brought their music to the new world settlement. The idea of these unique styles blending together to form something utterly new and distinctive took awhile to evolve. European musicians and song styles were to combine with African polyrhythms. This was a selection of musical roots that had never been combined before. At this point in time, the relocated Africans were not Americans yet. It was their arrival in North America, and their musical aptitude that would spark and kindle the new sound.

It should be noted that the slave trade existed on a worldwide level; it wasn't exclusive to the Confederate South. By the 1700s Africans had sold over twelve million Black people to Europeans as slaves, and seventeen million to Arabs. Slaves bound for North America were purchased on the West African coast in exchange for goods that were wanted by Black slave traders. The slaves were not acquired by white slavers raiding villages; that is a Hollywood myth. The compliance to a time when slavery was condoned is a moral sin; guilt must be shared by all the countries that were involved.

The interesting point here is that, although slavery was rampant throughout the world, it was only in North America that slaves were to change musical history by providing the missing ingredient that would inspire more than a new musical style, but a whole new category of music that would define a nation.

The musical traditions throughout Africa differed dramatically, both instrumentally and in concept, so much so as to be unrecognizable in different parts of that same continent. On the West African Coast, from where the slaves were being exported to North America, the music was composed of polyrhythms: several different rhythms played simultaneously. This was a culture that even used percussive rhythm for long distance communications. These polyrhythms differed from European rhythms and were part of the distinguishing ingredients that were to later make up jazz. Many of the polyrhythms were played off the beat and that made them syncopated. This feeling of syncopation was what would give us ragtime.

It was the original musical contribution of the West Coast African slaves combined with European musical styles and instrumentation that brought forth the creation of ragtime and jazz, and established a unique North American music.

The surprising thing is that, during all the cruelty and/or oppression the Black slaves endured, these generations of people remained very strong of mind and, upon reviewing many songs from this era, there is a surprisingly low percentage of songs expressing anger or resentment. This was a people that made the best of a situation. I also found that the contents of their songs relate mostly to their community, as if the White community was inconsequential. I believe it was this inner focus that gave them strength. It would be many years later, when the threat of retaliation was somewhat lessened, that the songs would give voice to injustice and oppression to be delivered as the blues, an idiom created for this very purpose.

To understand the conditions and turmoil that was slavery I recommend reading the fictional book, Uncle Tom's Cabin. This was written in 1830 and still stands up today, not with great posture, but it is upright. It was the bestselling novel of the 19th century and Abraham Lincoln acknowledged this book for fuelling and igniting the American Civil War. Hundreds of plays and theatrical productions were done of Uncle Tom's Cabin with no royalties paid to the author, Harriet Beecher Stowe.

While we are on the subject of slavery, and since it is seldom discussed, I thought I would throw in some additional information: Somehow history neglects to inform us about the Irish slave trade. It was not mentioned in any history classes that I attended. In the 1600s the majority of the early slaves to the New World were actually White.

The Irish slave trade started when James II of England began selling the Irish as slaves in the early 1600s. Over 600,000 Irish men, women and children were sold to the West Indies, Virginia, and New England. An African slave was ten times more expensive to purchase during the 1600s than an Irish one, partially because the Irish were harder to deal with and keep in line. The Irish musical contribution to the new music came in the form of a long standing traditional style which was marginally significant to the creation of the new music. But it was the Africans who stirred the pot and were creative enough to merge instrumentation and styles.

Below: Examples of slave cabins from the Southern American plantations. There would often be duplexes to house extended families. I found an original one at Louisiana's San Francisco Plantation.

Below: Replica slave cabins located at Oak Alley Plantation in Louisiana. The originals would have had a fireplace, and a fenced garden out back.

Importing off-shore slaves lasted in North America for over three hundred years; non-Black slavery already existed in the Americas by 1492 when Columbus landed. First Nations/Native American people had enslaved others captured from enemy tribes. African slaves were brought to

Spanish Florida as early as the 1560s. Florida was under Spanish rule at that time, as Louisiana was then under French rule. In the English colonies, Black slavery had its origins in Virginia in 1607. Slaves were brought to Canada as early as 1628. In Canada all slavery was ended in 1830, making Canada a safe haven for Black refugees until slavery was ended in the U.S. with the Thirteenth Amendment to the United States Constitution in 1865.

Before that change, the Underground Railroad referred to an organized group of brave and sympathetic U.S. and Canadian citizens who smuggled slaves from the Southern States over the border and into Canada. Here they could live as free refugees, with the option of applying for Canadian citizenship. This migration and new freedom allowed Black people the opportunity to access employment and enjoy the reward of receiving a paycheque. Some new arrivals decided to explore their musical talent and, in doing so, they influenced many of the local established musicians north of the border. These new found professional African- Canadian musicians could, for the first time in their lives, dedicate all their time to music, song, or dance. This focus of talent honed skills that would have perhaps never developed fully otherwise.

The grandson of a family that were former slaves, a man named Sheldon Brooks, born May 4, 1886 in Amherstburg, Ontario wrote "The Darktown Strutter's Ball" which was recorded in 1917 by the Original Dixieland Jass Band in the United States. The first two jazz songs in history were recorded that day and although The Darktown Strutter's Ball was the first to be recorded, it was the second song, "Livery Stable Blues" that was first released to the public. The first jazz record ever made and the first true jazz standard, The Darktown Strutter's Ball, was written by a Canadian composer. I am mentioning this to help instill the realization that this new music was a product that was influenced by many different elements of our North American culture. That song title needs explanation: there was German Town, China Town and Dark Town. Once slavery was abolished in the United States many of the free people of colour residing in Canada via the Underground Railroad returned to the United States to be with family and friends.

Work songs were chanted and sung by slaves. These songs were developed between the seventeenth and nineteenth centuries. They had an entirely oral culture and had no fixed form. They were not recorded in writing or otherwise until 1865, and then not by the people who had created them, but by those to whom they had been passed down to.

A common feature of African slave songs was the call-and-response format: a leader would sing a line or verse and the others would respond with a chorus. Here is a common example:

Caller: *All dem purty gals will be dar,*
Chorus: *Shuck dat corn before you eat.*

Caller: *They will fix it for us rare,*
Chorus: *Shuck dat corn before you eat.*

Caller: *I know dat supper will be big,*
Chorus: *Shuck dat corn before you eat.*

Caller: *I think I smell a fine roast pig,*
Chorus: *Shuck dat corn before you eat.*

Caller: *I hope dey'll have some whisky* dar,*
Chorus: *Shuck dat corn before you eat.*

Caller: *I think I'll fill my pockets full,*
Chorus: *Shuck dat corn before you eat.*

To make harvesting chores less monotonous slaves created songs to match the rhythm of the actions required to complete the harvest. Autumn for slaves meant additional labour associated with the harvest. This was the season when plantation masters were able to pay their debts and prepare the fields for spring planting. As an incentive, slaves were commonly promised special meals, rations of whisky*, and the opportunity to associate with slaves from other plantations in return for the quick completion of harvesting tasks.

"Hollers" were the workers on cotton farms and "Arhoolies" were the workers of wheat plantations, and they both developed work songs that were synchronized with the rhythm of their particular work. This call-and-response style was one of the elements that occasionally turns up in ragtime, jazz, and swing, both musically and verbally.

A good deal of the events regarding music, song, and show business that took place in the early 1800s were not written down until much later. This was often because the people involved were unable to write, or the momentum of the circumstances left the participants unaware of the possible historical value of their actions: chronicling names, conversations, and facts just didn't occur to anyone who was a participant at the time.

Songs and lyrics, especially the material that was created by the African slave community, was not written down as they were considered to be unworthy of documentation by those capable of writing music at the time. This Southern Slave Music, as it was described, was the forerunner and nucleus of much that would follow.

At this time, Blacks and Whites who were creating songs used the slang vernacular of the day in describing themselves and others. The words nigger, darky, coon, mammy, high-brown, and high-yellow are a few of the examples found within the lyrics of early songs. These terms, which today are considered to be derogatory, were just a common and acceptable part of everyday conversation in the early 1800s. As time progressed, particularly after the American Civil War when slavery was abolished, the slang vernacular describing African-Americans was recognized as inappropriate, and actions were taken by many citizens to no longer use this terminology. However, this accomplishment was slow coming. From the early 1880s to the mid 1920s several hundred "coon songs" were published and sold millions of copies. Jumping on the band wagon, many of the composers of coon songs were Black; they knew what would sell, and were willing to make the compromise to create the income.

After the Civil War, musicians realized all the songs written prior to 1865 were having the newly offensive words substituted with something more acceptable. Altering the original contents of the songs was stripping them of their roots, and was re-writing musical history. So the project was taken on to make a written copy of the original songs. At this time, many of the people who had created the songs were long dead, and the words and melody had been passed on many times before this opportunity surfaced to finally commit them to paper. The musical history in song form, the folk songs of America that are heard today, are not the original songs that were sung. Here is an example:

Today: (first verse only)
Title: Momma's Little Baby Loves Shortnin' Bread
Three little children lyin' in a bed,
Two was sick and the other most dead.
Sent for the doctor and the doctor said,
"Feed those children on shortnin' bread."
Momma's little baby loves shortnin', shortnin', Momma's little baby loves shortnin' bread.

The original song: (first verse)
Title: Mammy's Little Baby Loves Shortnin' Bread
Two little Niggers lyin' in a bed,
One was sick and the other near dead.
Call for the doctor an` de doctor said,
"Feed dem darkies on shortnin' bread."
Mammy's little baby loves shortnin', shortnin', Mammy's little baby loves shortnin' bread.

As you can see, the change had to be made, history erased and rewritten. I personally stand by the decision erased and rewritten, but I am a bit troubled by forgotten. Perhaps after enough time has passed the human race will have matured enough to be able to look back with honesty and acknowledge what took place.

Black people, being pure blood, were often distinguished by their different shade of skin colours, and they developed a code amongst themselves to help describe one another in conversation. In her 1942 Glossary of Harlem Slang, Zora Neale Hurston placed "high yaller" at the beginning of the entry for colour scale, which ran from lightest to darkest: "high yaller, yaller, high-brown, Vaseline-brown, seal-brown, low-brown, dark-brown". Interestingly, "black" was not a colour option.

An example of this usage is in the song "The Yellow Rose of Texas", written in 1836, author unknown. The lyrics are not clear in the modern version, but in the original they describe a light skinned woman of colour, and a black suitor.

Here is the original first line from the song:
There's a yellow rose in Texas, that I am going to see,
No other darky knows her, no darky only me.
Here is the first line from a rewritten modern version:
There's a yellow rose in Texas, I'm going home to see
Though other men have held her, her heart belongs to me.
Once again, rewriting these songs leave us with something somewhat different.

Slave Blood Mixes Categorized:
If you lived in Louisiana, originally a French colony eventually sold to the Spanish, and you could prove that you had a drop of French or Spanish blood in your ancestry, you could be considered a Creole and a free person of colour. Whereas, if you lived anywhere else in North America, and it could be proved that you had a drop of Black African blood in your ancestry, regardless of your appearance, legally you could be enslaved. Children from inter-racial couplings were categorized by the following terms:

Mulatto - was the offspring of a White person and a Black person
Mulatress - was a female Mulatto
Sambo - of a Mulatto and a Black person
Quadroon - is the offspring of a Mulatto and a White person
Mustee - is the child of a Quadroon and a White person (1/8th African ancestry). Sometimes called a Octoroon, or Terceron.
Mustefino - the child of a White person and a Mustee (1/16th African ancestory. Sometimes called a Quintroom or Hexadecaroon

With these definitions going that far back into a family's history, it made it possible for corrupt lawyers outside of Louisiana to procure or falsify lineage papers that could cause the arrest and enslavement of their enemies, or their client's enemies, even if the victim looked Norwegian.

CHAPTER TWO: THE MAKINGS OF THE MINSTREL SHOW

The first and most important concept in the creation of North American show business was the minstrel show. But before we can go there we need to chat a little about what influenced the first production.

Between 1750 and 1843, over 5,000 theatres and circus productions included a blackface performer. Blackface is the cosmetic application of burnt cork to the performer's face to represent a Black person. However, some historians credit the German singer Johann Graupner, who appeared in the Boston Theatre with cork-blackened face in 1799, as the first such performer.

The minstrel show, or minstrelsy, was an American entertainment concept consisting of comic skits, variety acts, dancing, and music, performed by White people in blackface or, after the Civil War, Black people in blackface. Negros put on blackface in order to gain the consistency of facial colour and, because it was like wearing a mask, it increased confidence and character. Makeup creates the feeling of taking on a persona, a theatrical character, and promotes free license to do and act not as yourself, but as your character, to enable and enhance the performer's artistic creativity.

Here are some of the stock characters used in minstrel show skits and dramatic performances:

Thomas Dartmouth Rice created a character called Jim Crow. It is said that he was copying a Negro stable hand that he saw down in a little river town who, while singing, would hop up in the air after each stanza and do a little dance. Thomas Rice took this character on the stage imitating the man's voice and appearing in blackface makeup. The costume was composed of soiled and torn ragged pants and shirt, a battered hat, and torn shoes. Rice made a living in 1827 performing in blackface and by 1830 the

Jim Crow character was his signature act. This was one of the ingredients that became a staple in minstrel shows. His act was so popular that within nine years there were hundreds of "Jim Crow" acts all over the North America.

Below: Image of Jim Crow

Another stock character found in skits in minstrelsy was Zip Coon. First performed by George Dixon in 1834, Zip Coon made a mockery of free Blacks. An arrogant, ostentatious figure, he dressed in high-style and spoke in a series of malaprops (misapplication of words) and puns that undermined his attempts to appear dignified.

Below: Image of Zip Coon

The Mammy was another dramatic minstrel character that was fiercely independent, accepting no backtalk. The stereotype lives on. This character can often be found on pancake boxes.

Below: The lovable Mammy character.

The "Uncle Tom" character, gentle and understanding, was a shoulder to lean on and a source of encouragement. Today that character, under the name of Uncle Ben, is still selling rice.

Pickaninnys were Black children with big black (later white) lips who were always eating watermelons.

Pictured is the famous child star: Billie Buckwheat Thomas.

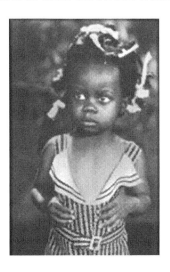

Buck was a flamboyant minstrel character who was typically a large Black man, occasionally menacing, and always interested in White women.

Below: the exuberant Buck.

The Jezebel or wench was always played by a Mulatto and, since minstrel shows didn't include female performers, a man or young boy would play the part.

Below: The flirtatious Jezebel

You can see an adaptation of the Jim Crow and Zip Coon characters in Amos and Andy: two Negro radio characters created and performed by two Caucasian comedians named Freeman Gosden and Charles Correll. Amos and Andy was the most popular radio show of all time.

Below: Freeman Gosden and Charles Correll:
Amos and Andy of radio fame.

Minstrel shows had proven to be so much a part of the entertainment world you can even see the influence in the original drawing of Mickey Mouse (blackface, white gloves, big yellow bow tie, and big buttons).

Minstrel shows lampooned Black people in mostly disparaging ways as ignorant, lazy, buffoonish, and superstitious. They were also portrayed as joyous and musical. The minstrel show began with brief burlesques and comic skits in the early 1830s and emerged in their full-fledged form in the following decade. The shows were performed with ignorance, but not intentional hatred. They were delivered as corn in the way that the T.V. show Hee-Haw lampooned country folks. The Black generation that inherited the right to contribute to minstrel show productions followed in suit.

Credit is given to Daniel Decatur Emmett for creating the initial formula that was to become the industry standard for minstrel show productions, and which was later improved upon by Christy's Minstrels. Daniel had been working as a printer in the winter and as a musician drummer in traveling circuses in the summer, though violin was his instrument of choice. It was during the tours in 1841 with the Cincinnati Circus that Daniel, now a banjo player, met the clown Frank Brower (sometimes mistakenly referred to as Frank Bower). Brower introduced bone playing, which he could do whilst simultaneously dancing and singing. He was a talented and respected performer. In the winter of 1842 instead of returning to the printing business in Cincinnati, Emmett joined Brower in a show at the Franklin Theatre in New York. William Whitlock and Richard Pelham came into the boarding house where Brower and Emmett were staying and, upon listening to the music Dan and Frank were making, settled in to play along. William played the banjo so Dan switched to his violin. Richard played his tambourine and with Frank playing bones and singing they soon realized that they were doing something special and unique.

Below: Dan Emmet's Virginia Minstrels performing at the Chatham Theatre in New York City in 1843.

Calling themselves Dan Emmett's Virginia Minstrels, their blackface revue followed up their Chatham Theatre premier with a performance at New York's Bowery Amphitheatre in February 1843. Dan Emmett (violin and banjo), Frank Brower (bones), Frank Pelham (tambourine) and Billy Whitlock (banjo) became the first troupe to offer a full evening of blackface variety entertainment. With their chairs in a simple semi-circle, the quartet offered a fresh combination of songs, dances, and comic banter, creating cartoonish caricatures. Most historians mark this production as the beginning of minstrelsy.

Dan Emmett created the formula that remained true throughout the years by creating the characters of Bruder Bones (playing bone castanets) and Bruder Tambo (playing the tambourine) as the end-men. He also created the traditional costume of the swallowtail coat, huge bow-tie and red pants. In 1859, it was Dan Emmett who wrote the song, Dixie's Land, later to be entitled, Dixie, while performing with the Bryant's Minstrels.

Below: Cover for song sheet of Dixie, by Dan Emmett.

It is interesting to note that the White men that were imitating the Black men dressed and danced like them, but it stops there. This theatrical farce used the Black slave's image, but the product and production was solely Caucasian. Here are some points to consider: All the songs used a European straight march beat, instead of the African drumming polyrhythm's and punctuated syncopation. Also, the melodic approach in minstrelsy used the verse-chorus structure, which is not heard in old-time Black music; all original Black music uses the call-and-response scheme (a single line followed by a repeated musical phrase).

So the white performers were giving the audience an identifiable musical product, while using the slave image, albeit a romanticized one. Such false idealism is seen in many lyrics of sentimental minstrel songs. In songs such as "Carry Me Back to Old Virginny" and "My Old Kentucky Home" Stephen Foster portrays the slaves as happy and singing all day with a love for their owners, even though they had to work hard. Another example is in the song "The Old Folks At Home":

All up and down the whole creation,
Sadly I roam,
Still longing for the old plantation,
And for the old folks at home.

White audiences were fed the notion that Blacks liked to be slaves and were content with their lives. This gave the White audience a clear conscience and a good excuse to not think about the fate of the oppressed Africans.

CHAPTER THREE: THE MINSTREL SHOW

Blackface minstrelsy was the first distinctly American theatrical form. In the 1830s and 1840s it motivated the rise of an American music industry, and for several decades it provided the lens through which White America saw Black America.

It had strong racist aspects, but it gave White Americans an awareness of significant aspects of Black-American culture. Unknowingly, it humanized the image of slaves and imprinted the needs and emotions that both communities had in common, thus developing, for the first time in the minds of the Caucasian audience, a sympathetic fondness and empathy for likable Black characters.

The typical minstrel performance followed a three-act structure. The opening act saw the troupe dance onto stage forming a semicircle, sometimes two or three layers deep depending on the number of cast members. They then performed the first musical number followed by the front row of the cast being seated. This was followed by songs and an exchange of wisecracks. The humour was thrown about by the end-men; the actors at the opposite far sides of the stage. The man at the audience's far left of the stage was seated and always called Bruder Tambo. He was the tambourine player and funny man. Seated on the audience's far right was Bruder Bones. He played bone castanets or spoons, and was the second part of the comedic end-men; the two of them contributed to the rhythm section. The other musicians would commonly play banjo, fiddle, and kazoo (at a later period horns were added). Seated up front, in the middle of all these blackface performers, was a man in whiteface called the Interlocutor (pronounced inter-lock-you-ter). He was the master of ceremonies and interrogator, often asking the end-men to explain themselves to which, in his pompous over-educated arrogance, it was obvious he had no idea what they were talking about. The audience loved to see someone "in power" be the butt of a joke. In later years, the first opening section would climax with a walk around dance similar to, or just like, the cakewalk.

After an intermission, the second section of the performance, called the Olio, was composed of popular songs and variety acts, and was performed in front of a painted backdrop. Its real purpose was to allow time to set the stage behind the backdrop for the one-act musical to follow in the third portion of the show. The olio is where we saw the birth of tap dancing. Some of the variety acts during this section were performed without blackface make-up, in part to prove to the audience that the performers were White. The last skit in the olio was often a "stump speech" given by one of the end-men. The humorous sarcasm poked fun at contemporary issues and political figures: this was the forerunner of stand-up comedy. The overall olio format would eventually evolve into vaudeville.

Following a second intermission was the one-act musical skit. These burlesqued (made fun of) a popular topic, novel, or play. Two of the stock blackface characters were always depicted: "Jim Crow", an ignorant country bumpkin ripe for humiliation, and his counterpart "Zip Coon", the city slicker whose self-assurance led to his comic come-uppance. Hateful to us today, these stereotypes were accepted as part of wholesome family entertainment in the 1800s. Both White and Black audiences embraced the songs and skits until minstrelsy disappeared. The one-act musical skits grew into the full-length Broadway "Burlesques" of the late1800s.

Blacks were not involved in minstrelsy until after the Civil War in 1865, at which time entire Black minstrel shows appeared using the same traditional format, characters and songs. They didn't want to tamper with a successful formula.

The music and song in the first twenty-five years of minstrel shows was not influenced by the African slave community, although minstrels claimed that their songs and dances were authentically Negro, the extent of the black influence remains debated. Often harmony was used on the minstrel stage adding more proof to the fact that there was very little in the way of influence by the early slave community. Spirituals known as "jubilees" entered the repertoire in the 1870s, marking the first undeniably black music to be used in minstrelsy.

In 1890 women began performing in minstrel shows for the first time and it increased the dramatic boundaries, whilst also providing for more depth to vocals and dance.

Some influential stars of the minstrel stage

Stephen Foster was the first American to become a full time professional song writer. He is known as the "Father of American Music." His songs were written for the minstrel stage and sold as sheet music (there were no phonograph records yet). They were played in homes all over the world. His compositions such as: "Oh! Susanna", "Camptown Races", "Old Black Joe", "Old Folks at Home" ("Swanee River"), "Hard Times Come Again No More", "My Old Kentucky Home", "Jeanie with the Light Brown Hair", and "Beautiful Dreamer" remain part of American history. Ironically, he was a Northern White man, who never lived in the South.

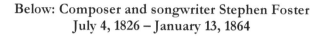

**Below: Composer and songwriter Stephen Foster
July 4, 1826 – January 13, 1864**

African-American minstrel show composer, James Bland created over 700 songs for the minstrel stage after the Civil War, and never managed to write down more than three dozen of his songs. His songs included "Carry Me Back to Old Virginny", "Oh, Dem Golden Slippers", and "In the Evening by the Moonlight."

Canadian minstrel show star Cool Burgess was known as "The Prince of Burnt-cork Comedians". He toured with all the major American minstrel shows and was a tremendous hit with his popular song, "Shoo, Fly! Don't

Bodder Me!"

Ted Healy was a minstrel who later went into vaudeville with an act he called Ted Healy and His Southern Gentlemen, a name he later changed to The Three Stooges.

In the 1840s, Christy's Minstrels, who were sometimes called The Christy Minstrels, were instrumental in adding the "Interlocutor" to the minstrel stage and also formulating the line-up in the first section of the three-act minstrel performance. The show would expand to eventually have over 200 performers on stage. It was Christy's Minstrels that hired young Steven Foster as their song composer. They were one of the greatest minstrel shows of all time.

E. Byron Christy was a son of Edwin Pearce Christy, founder of Christy's Minstrels. Byron was a comedian and was best known for his stump speeches. He played with his step-brother's troupe George Christy's Minstrels in 1859, after their return tour from California. In 1865 Christy's Minstrels made a tour under Byron's management. He died in New York City on April 6, 1866, at 28 years old.

William A. Christy, was the younger son of E. P. Christy. He was a comedian and a very good end-man, but his greatest skill was portraying female characters. Late in the 1860s Christy's Minstrels, under his management, toured for a brief season and closed. On July 4, 1861, they reorganized and opened at the Athenaeum, Brooklyn, N. Y. William A. Christy died in New York City, December 8, 1862. He was only 22 years old.

Billy Van began his career in minstrelsy at age 14. He contributed his artistic skills as performer, writer, vaudevillian, and burlesque comic. He worked the New York stage and also performed in silent movies. His stage career was to last 48 years.

Below: Billy Van, a minstrel star 1879 to 1927

George M. Cohan was doing blackface in 1881 and was the co-producer of the Cohan and Harris Minstrels which commenced performing in 1908 at the Apollo Theatre in Atlantic City, N.J.

The most famous minstrel star was the man who toured with Lew Dockstader's Minstrels: Al Jolson. Al was a star of minstrel, vaudeville, radio, and Broadway. He made several movies in blackface as a minstrel performer. Sophie Tucker, Eddie Cantor, Bob Wills, Bert Williams and Clarence Williams all worked the blackface minstrel stage.

Below: Al Jolson in blackface

Bert Williams was by far the best-selling black recording artist before 1920. In 1918 The New York Mirror called him, "one of the great comedians of the world." Bert Williams was the first black American to take a lead role on the Broadway stage. W.C. Fields, a fellow vaudevillian and friend, described him as "the funniest man I ever saw – and the saddest man I ever knew."

**Below: Bert Williams, a black entertainer in blackface
(1892 – 1922)**

At the end of the Gilded Age the minstrel show had lost momentum to be replaced by vaudeville which was so much less expensive to produce. However, amateur productions continued right up until 1960 in the Southern States.

CHAPTER FOUR: HISTORY OF DANCE

Dancing has always been immensely popular. I know that every dance that developed in North America will not be found on these pages, but here are some of the very notable ones that, if you are dance-crazy or hoof-nutty, you will want to know about.

The Cakewalk: In the mid 1800s, slaves in Florida combined their dance style with a coupled dance performed by native Seminole Indians. This dance was known as the Chalk Line Walk. I will tell you about the inspiration that would later turn this dance into the Cakewalk.

Below: The Cakewalk

The Cakewalk involved a promenade where participants would dance along a straight line in an exaggerated parody of the White upper-class and their distinctive Caucasian mannerisms. Essentially, this dance was created to make fun of the plantation owners and those who associated with them.

The White community, not quite in on the joke, thought the dance was tremendous fun and it became a national dance craze. By the 1890s the Cakewalk was one of the most popular dances around.

This was not just a dance but also a contest. The best dance couple would win a cake at the end of the evening when the judge would stand upon a table and point down at the winning couple, coining the phrase, "That takes the cake".

The Bunny Hug: In 1909 the Bunny Hug was danced to the popular ragtime hits of the day. This originated in San Francisco.

The Grizzly Bear: In the same year as the Bunny Hug, the Grizzly Bear was also danced to ragtime. This originated in San Francisco, too.

Turkey Trot: Created in the same year, in the same town, and danced to the same popular ragtime hits of the day as the previous two dances.

The Tango: This dance originated in the 1890s in the northern part of South America between Uruguay and Argentina. It is a partner dance that first became popular in the lower class districts of Montevideo and Buenos Aires. It was soon to become popular throughout Europe and, in 1913, it hit New York. As years went by different new tango steps were developed. For a short while the tenor banjo was referred to as the tango banjo. By 1930 the Tango had lost most momentum and fell from popularity altogether.

The Boston Dip: This was started in 1912, and by 1930 had achieved several names and transformed from a ragtime dance to a slow waltz. It was alternatively known as: The Imitative Boston, The Cradle Boston, The Spanish Boston, The Herring Bone Boston, The Long Boston, The Hesitation Boston, and The Philadelphia Boston.

The Shimmy: This was the first of the popular 1920s dance styles; it was a vulgar "cooch" dance, at its best. It appeared in musicals, danced by both sexes of the cast. Vaudeville, being more respectable, kept a wary eye on the Shimmy dancers on its stages. Curiously enough, the branch of show business that outlawed the Shimmy was burlesque (this was before burlesque had de-evolved from intellectual comedy to striptease).

Mae West brought down the house with the Shimmy in her 1921 show. The Shimmy was an exhibition dance only.

The Charleston: A form of The Charleston was performed as early as 1903, and it made its way to Harlem's stage productions by 1913. The Broadway show "Runnin' Wild", and another show titled "Shuffle Along" featured the Charleston with lyrics by Cecil Mack and music by James P. Johnson. It then appeared in cabarets, and was danced on stage by vaude and burly entertainers. It spread in popularity from the African-American community living near Charleston, South Carolina to become a nation-wide dance craze in 1923. As no dance before it, it went coast to coast with lightning speed. Even street entertainers were dancing in front of theatres for throw-money. The Charleston was the ultimate dance of the Roaring Twenties and a key element in the early evolution of swing dance.

The Charleston was ousted out of favour, after brief, but violent glory, by the Black Bottom of 1926. As quickly as The Charleston, the Black Bottom swept into vaudeville, burlesque, musical comedies, nightclubs, songs, and verse.

The Black Bottom (aka the Swanee Bottom): In 1926 this was the dance craze that took out the Charleston. Some say Alberta Hunter, the blues singer, was the first woman to present the dance commercially.

Apparently, The Black Bottom originated in New Orleans in the early 1900s. In 1919 the sheet music for the Black Bottom included instructions on how to perform the dance.

It was a lively dance that could be performed by a solo dancer or a dance couple. In its solo form, the Black Bottom resembled, and was the origin, of modern tap and jazz dancing. . It came from an earlier dance called "Jacksonville Rounders' Dance" created in 1907. The word "Rounder" was a synonym for "pimp." Both dance songs were written by pianist, composer, and dancer Perry Bradford, and were based on a dance done in Jacksonville, Florida. The theatrical show "Dinah" brought the Black Bottom dance to New York in 1924, and the George White's Scandals featured it at the Apollo Theater in Harlem in 1926 to 1927 where it was introduced by dancer Ann Pennington.

The Varsity Drag: Billy Pearce attempted to rival the success of The Black Bottom in 1927 with the Sugar Foot Strut, but it was too complicated for popular dancing. So were many other attempts such as The New Low Down and the Varsity Drag.

Sugar Foot Strut: 1928, see above.

Buck-and-Wing: This was a fast and flashy dance usually done in wooden soled shoes. It combined Irish clogging styles, high kicks, and complex African rhythms with steps such as the shuffle and slide.

The Foxtrot: The Foxtrot is a smooth progressive dance characterized by long, continuous flowing movements across the dance floor. Developed in the 1920s, The Foxtrot reached its height of popularity in the 1930s, and remains practiced today. It is danced to big band (usually vocal) music, and the feeling is one of elegance and sophistication. The dance is similar in its look to the waltz, although the rhythm is 4/4 instead of ¾ time.

Below: William Vernon and Irene Castle refined the Foxtrot
in Irving Berlin's first Broadway show "Watch Your Step" in 1914.

Below: Fred Astaire
In 1939 Fred made a movie with Ginger Rogers called,
"The Story of Vernon and Irene Castle".

The Big Apple: 1937 - The exact origin of the Big Apple is unclear but it could have originated from the "ring shout", a group dance associated with religious observances that was founded before 1860 by plantation slaves in South Carolina. The ring shout is described as a dance with "counterclockwise circling and high arm gestures" and it resembles the Big Apple.

The Lambeth Walk: The Lambeth Walk was originally a song from the 1937 musical "Me and My Girl". It became the name of a popular walking dance done in a jaunty strutting style that remained popular till 1942.

Swing Dance: Ever ask yourself how most of the musicians around 1935 were able to play swing music overnight like they had been playing it for years? Well...they had been playing it for years; it was just not commercially in demand. It was the "musician's music" and was more of an underground party sound. No one was recording it.

The very first known form of swing dance was the Texas Tommy which was danced in 1913; it later changed to the Mooch, and the Sugar dances in 1916. In 1919 it was called the Breakaway, but during the 1920's, when The Charleston was becoming all the rage, the Breakaway and Charleston would start to mix and form a new unnamed dance style. In 1927 this style was finally acknowledged and named by a swing dancer named George "Shorty" Snowden. Shorty George, from New York's Harlem, re-named the Breakaway and called it the Lindy Hop or Lindbergh Hop, after the pilot Charles Lindbergh successfully completed a thirty-three hour flight across the Atlantic Ocean to France on May 20, 1927.

Here's how it happened: In September 1927, a newspaper reporter interviewed the winners at a dance contest in Central Park in New York. He asked the winning couple, Shorty George and The Big Bea, what was the dance they were doing, as he had not seen it before. Shorty thought for a second and replied "the Lindy Hop...We flying just like Lindy did!" The newspaper reporter did an article in his newspaper and described what he saw, calling it the Lindy Hop.

The Black community was dancing the Lindy fast, but very smooth and cool; the style was unique. The White college kids, in an attempt to make it theirs, were stiffer and lacked the elegance seen in Harlem. These kids called it the Jitterbug. Jitter was a Black slang word that meant liquor, and a jitterbug was someone who drank liquor.

The Savoy Ballroom: On March 12, 1926 the doors opened at the Savoy. It was billed as "The World's Finest Ballroom", located at 596 Lenox Avenue in Harlem, NYC. The dance floor was 200 feet long and 50 feet wide. It had two bandstands and a retractable stage. It was the most popular dance venue in Harlem during an age when all of Harlem danced. The Savoy Ballroom was host to all the great talents of early jazz and swing. Over the years, bandleaders such as Cab Calloway, Chick Webb, Count

Basie, and Duke Ellington would trade sets from opposite bandstands in the Savoy's well known "Battle of the Bands." And while the bands battled, the dancers competed to out-dance one another. Three of greatest dance couples in Harlem were: "Twistmouth" George Ganaway and Edith Matthews, Leroy "Stretch" Jones and Little Bea, and "Shorty" George Snowden and The Big Bea.

CHAPTER FIVE: NORTH AMERICAN BURLESQUE

Most people see burlesque as the bump and grind of scantily dressed, tassel twirling strippers seducing an audience with charm, sexual allure, and thoughts of the forbidden. This was not the original formula for burlesque, and in North America we were to see the production trends changing and evolving to the will of public demand and financial pressure.

In its original form the theatrical enticement and artistic skill displayed was often enhanced by, or over-shadowed by humour, an element of shock, or a dramatic or theatrical surprise: it was this that kept you in your seat wondering what will come next. This was an art that had survived since the 1600s in Europe, but had taken on a new personality in North America where it was most popular from 1860 to 1940.

It was once a rich source of comedy and music that enraptured the public with laughter and excitement. Burlesque was similar to vaudeville, but with the addition of sexual innuendo. The stage was graced with multitalented performers who challenged the politics of the day, and provided spoofs and caricatures of speeches, as well as plays and modern song. For the amusement of people in the middle and lower income brackets, early burlesque provided a parody of what life was like for the elite upper-class.

Burlesque from the 1800s involved scantily dressed women in an age when most women hid their physical form beneath bustles, hoops, and frills. Nudity was never an option until much later. The performance was suggestive rather than bawdy, and displayed its performance strength in strong song and well written script. By the 1880s the industry had slipped from the hands of thespians, and became controlled by male management. The program was shifting to involve as much tease as they could get away with, without crossing the line into vulgarity. Comedy was a huge selling card and the top male comic in a show provided a stimulant for ticket sales, and usually shared the biggest amount of the show's profit. Some very impressive names started out in burlesque: Jackie Gleason, Fanny Brice, Leon Errol, Mack Sennett, Bert Lahr, W.C. Fields, Bobby Clark, Red Skelton, Phil Silvers, Joey Faye, and Bob Hope. Most of these performers went on to musical comedy, radio, television, and movies.

Gypsy Rose Lee was born in Seattle, Washington in 1911 as Rose Louise Hovick. As a young girl she worked in vaudeville, but lacked the talent to do very well in that arena. She switched to burlesque where she produced a classy and witty striptease act. It is said that one of her shoulder straps on her dress accidentally broke during her performance, causing her dress to fall to her ankles. This brought her sharp sense of humor into play and the audience loved it. She reproduced this accident as part of her show and the audience came back time and again. She was the creator of the smooth casual style striptease. She changed her name to "Gypsy Rose Lee" and was one of the biggest stars of "Minsky's Burlesque". She performed with the show for four years and went on to movies, radio, and became a screenplay writer in the forties.

Below: autographed promo picture of Gypsy Rose Lee.

In the 1920s, with the advance of the depression and the onslaught of prohibition, burlesque circuits closed down. In desperation, individual burlesque houses introduced the striptease in an effort to provide something that vaudeville, radio, and film could not. Eventually, the strippers dominated burlesque, and any other performance was just in the way of seeing more nudity. However, showing too much could potentially land them in jail for corrupting public morals. Some police departments were content with G-strings and pasties as frontline cover-ups, but eventually the general public had had enough, and the crackdowns were enacted with raids, arrests, and closures. As hardcore pornography became readily available, men turned away from visiting the sleazy environments into which burlesque had evolved.

Burlesque is now making a small resurgence. It will never see the fame that once was, and today's reproduction is accomplished more for the entertainer's experience and sense of empowerment than from public demand and, although truthful in its attempts to be original and camp, the lack of financial backing and production values denies it any chance to compete in the contemporary market.

CHAPTER SIX: BARBERSHOP QUARTETS

In the 19th century the barbershop was much more than a place to get a haircut. It was a social gathering centre for men; it was where the guys hung out; an undeclared men's club. It was very common in an age, where there was very little in the way of entertainment, for people to sing songs together. Today the suggestion would seem awkward, but in the 1800s singing together was a typical social activity!

In 1870 the song style that was to be known as Barbershop Harmony or Curbstone Harmony became very popular. It was referred to as Curbstone Harmony because it was sung on the street corner as often as it was sung inside the barbershop. Different barbershops would compete against one another in town events. It, of course, was also well received at private social functions, fairs, and festivals.

A Barbershop society was created in 1938 in Oklahoma to promote the longevity of Barbershop Quartets. The Barbershop Harmony Society is legally and historically named the "Society for the Preservation and Encouragement of Barbershop Quartet Singing in America Inc." (SPEBSQSA).

Since then, barbershop societies have been developed in Britain, Australia, Canada, Ireland, and New Zealand.

Today, the word "barbershop" is used to describe both men's and women's quartets singing in the barbershop style. Harmony Inc. calls itself "International Organization of Women Barbershop Singers". Sweet Adelines International calls itself "A worldwide organization of women singers committed to advancing the musical art form of barbershop harmony."

Below: "Mixed Company" a modern day Barbershop Quartet from Greater Vancouver, British Columbia, performing in a vaudeville show co-produced by the author.

CHAPTER SEVEN: MEDICINE SHOWS AND PITCH MEN

You should know that there is no correlation between medicine show performers and pitch men. Pitch men (also known as badge dodgers) were crooks who would deceive the public and leave in the night. They worked without licenses or permits, and always for personal gain.

The medicine show, now that was a different thing altogether. Sometimes (quite often) the elixir, tonic, medical ointment, vegetable pills, sarsaparilla, salve or ointment was as phony as a three dollar bill. But the entertainment that preceded and followed the sales was well worth the cost.

Medicine shows went to small, out of the way towns that could never, for lack of venue and numbers of customers, attract a minstrel show, circus, or any type of vaudeville performance. These remote audiences were starved for entertainment. The best thing that happened in their town was the yearly spelling bee. The medicine show was welcomed with open arms. It would arrive with an entertainment section to gather the crowd to which the medicine man could sell his wares. People could expect to see dancing, storytelling, magic, music, and comedy acts.

There were legitimate medicine companies that would hire a traveling troupe of performers and a salesman (doctor) who would sell their product town to town, and stock the local drug store for after-sales. There were also legitimate medical companies like Frank P. Home's German Medicine Company which supplied over one hundred independent medicine shows with genuine products that would provide real results. These medicines were sold to the traveling "doctors" at cost. The manufacturer's profit came from the drug stores that purchased enough stock to last for years thereafter. Selling a well known German medicine gave legitimacy to the vendor who would sometimes sell additional items during and after the show. These would range from mirrors, pencils, household items, make-up, picture postcards, dime-novels, and pulp magazines.

Below: The good doctor pitching his "miracle tonic".

In the year 1902, ninety percent of medical doctors in North America hadn't attended college. One of the big sales items made available in traveling medicine shows was "soothing syrups." In this era people were simply too busy churning butter, waxing their moustaches, or changing in and out of fourteen layers of frilly undergarments every time they needed to urinate, to be bothered with disobedient children. Coming to the aid of the stressed Victorian mother was a series of soothing syrups. The most popular was "Mrs. Winslow's Soothing Syrup", guaranteed to transform a teething, cantankerous toddler into a smiling happy child content to just sit quietly. Such concoctions contained one or any combination of: morphine, chloroform, codeine, heroin, opium, and/or cannabis.

Below: Each ounce of Mrs. Winslow's Soothing Syrup contained 65 mg of pure morphine.

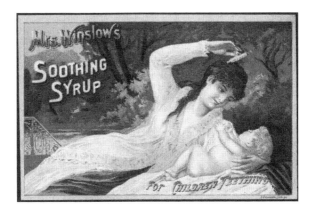

The medicine show would arrive and the wagon would open up producing an elevated stage from which to hawk the products and have the entertainers perform. Sometimes they would rent a local barn or warehouse if it looked like rain. The medicine shows were not fly-by-night. They would often stay for an entire week in a larger town or city. Occasionally medicine shows would travel by rail car, and, after WW1, by truck pulling a stage-trailer.

Some of the companies would have several wagons out in different towns at the same time, the largest of such being The Kickapoo Indian Medicine Show. The head office, called the "Principal Wigwam and Factory" (est. 1881) where they made the medicines, was located in Connecticut. It was owned by two Caucasians and had nothing to do with the real Kickapoo Indian Nation which existed in Oklahoma. The company provided housing for the entertainers and workers that comprised the twenty-five traveling medicine shows selling Kickapoo Medicine.

Here is an example of the sales pitch used in a Medicine Show by the author himself:

"Ladies and gentlemen, boys and girls of all ages, step right up for the education that may save your life!

How much is your health worth? I have come here today with one thought in mind; to make this a healthy and disease free town. Let me introduce you to the most important investment of your life, Dr. West's Miracle Tonic!

This will cure rheumatism, cancer, diabetes, baldness, bad breath, curvature of the spine, and female problems. Also it will cure coughs, colds, lumbago, corns, bunions and croup, blackheads, whiteheads, redheads, and blondes. It will rid you of cockroaches, ants, uncles, and other household pests. Perfect for neuralgia, kidneys, stomachs, and kids that you can't stomach. It makes hens lay more eggs, cows give more milk, and butterflies more butter. Gentlemen! Do you fear losing your manly powers? Stop taking tonics, ointments and vitality pills and insist on no substitutions! Dr. West's Miracle Tonic can cure every ailment known to man. It will reduce inflammation, reverse castration, increase your smile, eliminate bile, worms and warts. Having trouble touching your toes? That's why God gave you knees! Gas, gout and gum disease will be a thing of the past. This will cure and eliminate excess fat, body odour and canker sores. Say goodbye to hearing loss, dry skin and pinkeye. You will never experience rickets, wrinkled skin or tuberculosis. No more puffy eyes, polyps or parasites. Dr. West's Miracle Tonic: the product that makes childbirth a pleasure!"

Below: The author accompanied by Miss Jennifer Macdonald in Dr. West's Travelling Medicine Show era 1990s. (The name was respectfully borrowed from its originator, Mr. Norman Greenbaum).

Medicine shows sometimes included freak shows, flea circuses, musical acts, storytelling, magic tricks and jokes. The performers would move on after a few years and join up with a different medicine show circuit. This allowed the companies to provide fresh shows and avoid the chance of audiences losing their enthusiasm. Harry Houdini, Buster Keaton, and P.T. Barnum all did their time with med shows.

The man known as the "World's Greatest Medicine Show Operator" was Thomas Patrick Kelley. Also known as "Doc Kelley", he was born April 14th, 1865 (the night Lincoln was shot) in Ontario. In 1881, at age16, he formed his first med show. Kelley had a seven-act show needing at least two wagons to move it around. He would stay in one town for as much as two to eight weeks at a time, and when Kelley departed he left behind bottles of his cure-alls which sold steadily for years to follow in the drug store. Kelley made over two million dollars during his career as a medicine show proprietor. Some audiences were estimated to be over six-thousand per night. For more information, read the book "The Fabulous Kelley" by Thomas P. Kelley Jr. (his son).

Actual patents for medicine were not legalized until 1925. A law was passed in 1932 directing manufacturers to test their products for safety.

I found a label with the ingredients from a cough syrup bottle which read: Alcohol, morphine, cannabis, chloroform and sulfur, skillfully combined with a number of other ingredients.

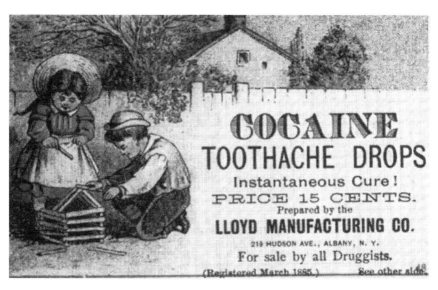

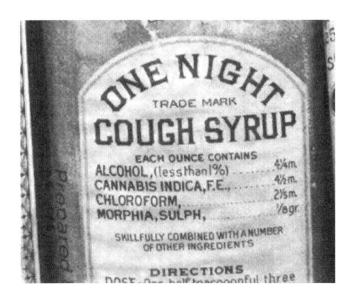

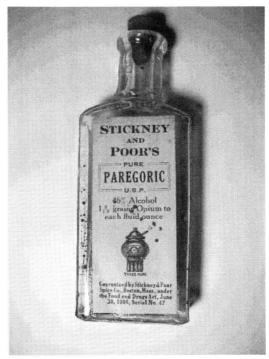

**Below: Asthma cigarettes,
not recommended for children under 6 years (very sensible!)**

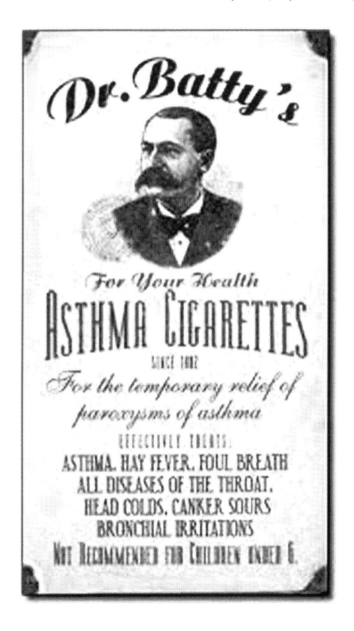

CHAPTER EIGHT: WILD WEST SHOWS

In the early 1870s Wild Bill Hickok - army scout, gunfighter, marshal, sheriff, and legendary frontier star of dime-novels and pulp magazines - opened his own Wild West show called *The Daring Buffalo Chase of the Plains*. Due to poor management and lack of skilled production, the show did not do well and eventually folded.

In December 1872, William Frederick Cody ("Buffalo Bill") traveled to Chicago to make his stage debut with friend Texas Jack Omohundro in *The Scouts of the Prairie*. This, too, was one of the original Wild West shows, and produced by Ned Buntline. During the 1873-74 seasons, Cody and Omohundro invited their friend, James Butler "Wild Bill" Hickok, to join them in a new play called *Scouts of the Plains*. It is said that the contract Hickok signed to take part in this Wild West show stated that he had to stop killing people while in the employment of the show.

The show was produced to be performed inside of theatres, and the atmosphere of city life became depressing for Hickok. During one of their productions, word on the street was that the local tough guys at a saloon nearby were talking loudly about "kicking the tar out of those Wild West heroes in the theatre." To avoid the bad press, Buffalo Bill told Hickok, and everyone else in the show, to enter by the back door of the theater that night.

Hickok had been on a hard drinking binge. He claimed to be leaving early from their hotel to grab some food on the way to the show. However, he went straight to the saloon and kicked the doors open, walked into the middle of the room and shouted, " I'm Wild Bill Hickok. Anyone want to kick my ass?" Hickok left the saloon in time to enter through the rear door of the theatre for the performance. The saloon he had left was riddled with the bleeding, unconscious bodies of the toughest men in New York. This held his depression off for about a week.

But, ultimately Hickok wanted out of his contract. "I want to go back out west where I can kill a man if he makes me mad." Hickok continued drinking and, guns loaded, he was shooting the footlights out on the theatre's stage regularly enough that the contract was finally torn up and he left on great terms with everyone. They still loved him; he was just too hard a man for city life. Wild Bill never returned to performing in Wild West shows.

Below: Wild Bill Hickok

It was May of 1883 when Bill Cody was able to leave the theatre to pursue his dream of an open-air Wild West performance: his own show. The first production ran in the fairgrounds in Omaha. He called it *The Wild West, Rocky Mountain and Prairie Exhibition*. The show featured marksmanship with Cody shooting on horseback at a full gallop; there was also a stagecoach attack, a Pony Express demonstration, horse races, steer riding, and a finale called the Grand Hunt of the Plains. This featured buffalo, elk, mountain sheep, longhorns, deer, and wild horses. After that first run, the show went on the road and was a great success.

Below: Buffalo Bill Cody

Frank Butler, a well known sharpshooter, arrived in town as an exhibition marksman and he issued an open challenge to local sharpshooters to compete. A local hotel owner had backed a young girl named Annie Oakley. Frank thought someone was playing a joke on him when Annie arrived wearing her pink gingham dress and her big sunbonnet. Blowing kisses to the crowd she picked up a rifle and, in a very few minutes, had won both the contest and the heart of Frank Butler. A year later they were married.

Annie was so much better than Frank, so much better than anyone, that Frank retired from competition and was happy being her manager. When the couple first saw *Buffalo Bill's Wild West* they loved it, and they joined the show in Louisville. Annie Oakley was a little lady, not the tough tomboy that many think she must have been. No one could out shoot her and there are short films that can be viewed on the internet (if you look hard enough for them) of her marksmanship. It is worth the trouble of finding these to see her shoot a dime out from between a man's thumb and index finger, shoot playing cards thrown into the air, shoot a cigarette out of someone's mouth, or throw two targets up into the air, jump over a table, pick up a rifle and shoot the targets before they could hit the ground. The camera man in these films was Thomas Edison.

As *Buffalo Bill's Wild West* developed, Buffalo Bill and his performers began to include re-enactments of Indian attacks on wagon trains, and stagecoach robberies. The show typically ended with a melodramatic re-enactment of Custer's Last Stand in which Cody himself portrayed General Custer.

During the winter of 1886 the show moved indoors to Madison Square Garden. Featuring Native Americans, trick riders, "the smallest cowboy", and sharpshooters (including Annie Oakley). It is said to have drawn millions of visitors.

In 1887, he took the show to Britain in celebration of the Jubilee year of Queen Victoria. The show was staged in London before going on to Birmingham, and then Salford for five months. They continued abroad to tour Europe in 1889. In 1890 he met Pope Leo XIII.

Upon returning to the U.S.A, he set up an exhibition near the Chicago World's Fair of 1893, which greatly contributed to his popularity and pocket book; it also angered the promoters of the fair. As noted in a local publication, his request had been refused to be part of the fair, so he set the show up just to the west of the fairgrounds, drawing many of their patrons away. Since his show was not part of the fair, he was not obligated to pay the promoters any royalties.

Here are some of the performers featured in *Buffalo Bill's Wild West*: Wild Bill Hickok, Annie Oakley, Calamity Jane, Will Rogers, Tom Mix, Chief Sitting Bull, Geronimo, Pawnee Bill, James Lawson, Bill Pickett, Mabel Croan, Jess Willard, Mexican Joe, Capt. Adam Bogardus, Buck Taylor,

Ralph and Nan Lohse, Antonio Esquibel, and Capt. Waterman and his Trained Buffalo, Johnny Baker "Cowboy Kid", and Rains-In-Face (who reportedly was General Custer's killer).

**Below left: Calamity Jane Top right: Geronimo
Bottom right: Will Rogers**

Below left: Pawnee Bill, Bill Cody, and unknown
Below right: Chief Sitting Bull and Bill Cody.

The show progressed through the years; performers and acts changed to keep it fresh. It would open with a parade on horseback. The parade was a major spectacle, an affair that involved huge public crowds and many performers, including, on some occasions, the Congress of Rough Riders. The Congress of Rough Riders was composed of marksman from around the world including the future president of the United States, Theodore Roosevelt (Teddy's Rough Riders). Each show was three to four hours long and attracted crowds of thousands of people daily.

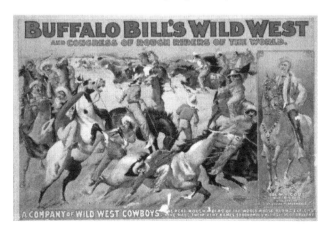

Fluctuations in the line-up included acts known as The Bison Hunt, Train Robbery, Indian War Battle Reenactment, and the grand finale used in some of the shows: Attack on the Burning Cabin, in which Indians attacked a settler's cabin and were repulsed by Buffalo Bill, cowboys, and Mexicans.

Below: Reenactment of Custer's Last Stand (1905)

Animals also did their share in the show through rodeo entertainment, an audience favorite. In rodeo events, cowboys like Lee Martin would try to rope and ride broncos. Broncos are unbroken horses that attempt to throw their riders. Other animals in the production were mules, buffalo, Texas steers, elk, deer, bears, and moose.

William F. Cody died of kidney failure on January 10, 1917, surrounded by family and friends at his sister's house in Denver. He is credited with helping to create and preserve a lasting legend of the West.

The musical *Annie Get Your Gun* is loosely based on the lives of Annie Oakley and Frank Butler. On the 3rd of November 1926 Annie Oakley died. Just two weeks after her death on the 21st of November 1926, Frank died.

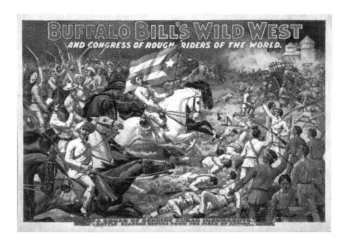

Pawnee Bill was Gordon W. "Pawnee Bill" Lillie, born on February 14, 1860. *Pawnee Bill's Wild West Show* started in 1888, and was highly successful. Twenty years later, when Buffalo Bill's show started to suffer financially in 1908 Pawnee Bill purchased 1/3rd interest in *Buffalo Bill's Wild West*. Soon, Gordon bought the remaining interest in the show, but retained Buffalo Bill as an operating partner.

Below: Poster advertising The Pawnee Bill Wild West Show

The two traveled together as *The Two Bill's Show* and their venture was billed as one of the entertainment triumphs of the ages, traveling all over the world entertaining audiences with both realistic and fantastical views of the Old West. The project eventually went bankrupt because expenses for an ever expanding, lavish production exceeded the profits. The show closed in Denver, Colorado in 1913 after touring for five seasons.

In 1930 Pawnee Bill built and operated *Pawnee Bill's Old Town*, two miles west of his ranch. This was a tourist attraction featuring log cabins, tepees, saloons, gunfights, and other attractions from the Old West. Six years later his wife, May Manning, died in an automobile accident. Gordon died in 1942. He was 81.

Other Wild West shows include: *Captain Baldwin's Wild West Show*, *Captain Jack Baldwin's Wild West Show*, *Texas Jack's Wild West Show* and *The Miller Brother's 101 Ranch Wild West Show*.

CHAPTER NINE: VAUDEVILLE

Before radio, television, and movies there were vaudeville companies whose corporate management structure remains in place today. Loew's theatres, MGM, 20th Century Fox, Paramount, and RKO: these were all companies founded by vaudeville producers.

Vaudeville was a variety show that followed a formula designed to entertain an audience with act after act. If you were not certain that you liked what was on stage at the moment, it didn't matter, because in five minutes a different performer would give you their best. It was the first major North American institution to offer serious opportunity for professional advancement, no matter a person's race, sex, or religion, and that gave the public a liberating feeling.

The word vaudeville became common after 1871 with the formation of *Sargent's Great Vaudeville Company* of Louisville, Kentucky. Louisville can be credited as the birthplace of several entertainment concepts.

October 24th 1881: Tony Pastor creates the first "clean show". Tony - considered "the Father of Vaudeville" - had begun his career in the circus as a singing clown and acrobat, and later worked in minstrel shows. In 1881 Tony Pastor, who had earned quite a name for himself as a singer and performer, realized that if he could make the performance clean he might be able to include women and children in his audiences. With the opportunity to more than double his income he produced what he advertised as "polite variety programs". The shows were in such demand that he ran them back to back and real vaudeville was born.

Later, Benjamin Franklin Keith and his partner, stage manager Edward Franklin Albee ran with the idea and turned it into a monopoly. Buying out independent theatres, they created an empire of performance houses and took control of the industry.

**Below: Benjamin Franklin Keith
and Edward Franklin Albee**

And boy! were they strict: when they said play clean, they meant it. If you disobeyed their rules you got one warning. Once more and you were black-listed and would never work again in a Keith-Albee house. This meant that you were finished in vaudeville.

Warnings were posted backstage in all of Keith & Albee's theatres. (Keith was the owner, Albee was the manager)

Here is an example:

"Don't say "slob" or "son of a gun" or "hully gee" on the stage unless you want to be canceled peremptorily. Do not address anyone in the audience in any manner. If you do not have the ability to entertain Mr. Keith's audience with risk of offending them, do the best you can. Lack of talent will be less open to censure than would be an insult to a patron. If you are in doubt as to the character of your act consult the local manager before you go on stage, for if you are guilty of uttering anything sacrilegious or even suggestive you will be immediately closed and will never again be allowed in a theatre where Mr. Keith is in authority."

"Everyone Play Clean": nothing sexual or off-colour could be on the vaudeville stage.

Between the Monday matinee and the evening show, the blue envelopes would begin to appear in the performers' mailboxes backstage. Inside would be a curt order to cut a questionable piece of business within a routine. Sometimes there was a suggestion of something to be substituted for the material the manager ordered cut . . . There was no arguing about the orders in the blue envelopes. They were final. You obeyed them or quit. And if you quit, you got a black mark against your name in the head office and you didn't work on the Keith Circuit anymore.

Thanks to the tint of those dreaded envelopes, anything off coloured became known as "blue" material.

This was a time in North American history where the average factory worker did a ten hour day, six days a week, for about $600.00 to $700.00 yearly. A vaudeville performer, with mediocre skills, could work consistently, and would make three times that much in a season. The call to the stage was a loud one.

In the age of vaudeville the term "manager" did not refer to people who managed acts or performers. The only managers that mattered managed the business that was vaudeville. In the last two decades of the 19th century, a handful of men created a formula for extracting each and every penny out of audiences, from what had previously been a fly-by-the-seat-of-your pants business.

Pioneering morning-to-night, back-to-back performances of "continuous vaudeville", they compartmentalized the mass of variety performers into useful categories, shifting them from show to show around the country on rigid time-tables to comply with their nationwide theatre circuits, in order to utilize their every moment while under contract. The industry they created was so tightly run, and so closely monitored, nothing took place that was not under their control. This produced a period in our history with more entertainers working than at any other time.

Here is how it worked: (This is the formula folks.)

Eight or nine acts became the industry standard. However, sometimes there were as many as twenty-one acts. The opening act was a throwaway: never exciting, nor too interesting, always dull, usually an animal act or acrobats, and was known as a "dumb act". It was to cause people to take their seats and get the show underway.

The next act was really considered the opener, and was referred to as the "doormat". This was doing the same job that movie trailers do in theatres today: people will always come in late.

The following act was considered "the deuce spot" and was the position typically reserved as a tryout spot for new acts. You were likely to see a singing-sisters act or dancing-brothers act, a male-female song and dance team, or maybe just an up-and-coming singer. It was also known as "the burying ground" because so many acts died there.

Number three was usually a flash act, a large production with sets and a big cast, designed to finally snap the audience out of their stupor. Maybe a magic act, or a comedy sketch, or a one-act play with a full set.

The fourth act was intended to hit the crowd right between the eyes. This was to carry the momentum right through to the main act. Usually a popular singer, or a novelty act, or comedy team.

Five would be a headliner so as to keep the audience buzzing through the intermission. Because the "top headliner" would get the next to the closing spot, the fifth position went to someone rising or declining, to or from fame.

-Intermission-

The very tricky sixth spot would have the job of settling the audience down again following intermission, while matching the energy built up by the fifth act...yet without outclassing the acts in the seventh or eighth slots. The classiest of "dumb" acts would work here. Perhaps a comedy juggler, a ballet dancer, or a musician.

A full stage act would go on seventh, something on a scale to awe beyond the spectacles in the third and fifth slots. Usually a musical outfit such as a novelty orchestra would take this spot.

The coveted next-to-closing slot would be the main headliner, usually the most popular comedian, singer, or comedy team.

Ninth and last was the "haircut act" or "chaser". This often well paid act was something so terrible, so appalling, it would have the audience heading for the door. All the performer would see was the back of people's heads as they walked out.

Step ten, do it all over again.

The full show ran continuously from 10:00 A.M. to 11:00 P.M. You could arrive anytime and stay until it started to repeat itself in order to see the entire show.

Despite their expectations that the acts perform clean, management was very aware of the "sex sells" rule. But, how to go there and not be detected? Instead of allowing sexual innuendo aimed at gentlemen, which would be immediately recognized by female audience members for exactly what it was, the inclusion of sexual allure was aimed at women. The Victorian woman could feign ignorance, whilst enjoying the arousing performance!

Jules Leotard, acrobat, appeared on stage in a trapeze act dressed in the very revealing "leotard" he invented. Women went wild! After the performance, which was staged as "art", he would go to a private room off stage where women could come in and inspect him by touch to "reassure" themselves that he was real and not aided by any mechanical device, as his performance was said to be so shockingly impossible that no ordinary man could do it. It was about him that the song "The Daring Young Man on the Flying Trapeze" was written. The line-up for this opportunity to personally inspect him would cause the theatre to stay open well after the show's finale.

An act could be darn near anything that was inoffensive and entertaining. A performer's gender, race, and appearance were no barrier to success, and nothing was too eccentric if it gave an audience ten to fifteen minutes of diversion. While singers and dancers were part of every bill, the specialty acts set vaudeville apart: mind readers, instrumentalists, escape artists (Houdini and his many imitators), flash acts (any "showy" act boasting its own lavish set), a large chorus, high divers, quick-change artists, strong men, living statuary, contortionists, balancing acts, freak acts - anyone acting crazy or silly - eccentric dancers, regurgitaters - these individuals drank liquids and then brought them back up to fill fish tanks and more.

Below: Hadji Ali would swallow water & kerosene, then spew kerosene onto open flames, followed by the water to put the flames out. Not pretty, but audiences were fascinated.

Below: Harry Houdini, world's foremost escapologist.

Acrobats, ice and roller skaters, cyclists, and other non-talkers were known as "dumb acts." A few of these went on to stardom when they added humourous repartee to their routines, including juggler W.C. Fields and rope trickster Will Rogers. Think-a-Drink Hoffman came onstage with an empty cocktail shaker and somehow made it pour forth any alcoholic concoction audience members called for. A few unique acts defy definition.

The Palace Theatre was the ultimate vaudeville house in which to perform. It was open from 1913 to 1929, located at 1564 Broadway (at 47th) in Manhattan. This was where everybody wanted to play.

Below from left: The Marx Brothers

Below: The Three Stooges

Below: Abbot and Costello

Below: Jack Benny

Below: top left to right: Jimmy Durante, Fred Allen
bottom left to right: Buddy Rich, George Burns and Gracie Allen.

**Below: top left to right: Mae West, Clara Bow,
bottom left to right: W.C. Fields, Al Jolson.**

Vaudeville has many relatives: The Medicine Show; the Circus with its emphasis on clowns, acrobats, trained animals, the back lot, popcorn and lemonade; the Dime Museum – which laid way to the sideshow, with its freaks, junk science, and lurid displays of the stillborn; and of course the Minstrel Show, a three part performance hinged on the unifying element of its problematic impersonation of Black plantation workers; the English music hall, with its emphasis on bawdy and sentimental song; and the Chautauqua, a highbrow variety show.

CHAPTER TEN: CHAUTAUQUA

1874 – 1940 was the heyday of Chautauqua ("sha-TAW- kwa"). It is an adult education movement in the United States; a sort of highbrow variety show combining lectures, poetry, music recitals, and genteel humour. All these forms were performed in a wide range of venues from taverns, inns, and saloons, to riverboats and legitimate theatres.

It began on the shores of Chautauqua Lake in 1874 and was originally organized by a Methodist minister, John Heyl Vincent and a businessman, Lewis Miller. It started as a summer school and grew to take on permanent residences in major cities, educating while entertaining the public.

Today the Chautauqua is once more alive and well in the United States and you can attend the free live performances where you will witness re-enactors portraying historical figures who give speeches and allow the audience to ask questions and receive answers from the likes of Mark Twain, Patrick Henry, Clara Barton, Harry Truman, and Robert Smalls.

Below: On the grounds of the Chautauqua Institution in New York, The Athenaeum Hotel, built in 1881. It has 156 rooms and is possibly the largest wood-structure building in the Eastern U.S.

CHAPTER ELEVEN: OLA AND COLA

One might well question the need for discussion concerning the Ola-Cola dilemma.

In response, I can only say that entertainers and the general public were affected by the contents of these beverages and, well, I just think it's interesting. I think you will too.

Some of the early soda pop beverages (and believe me, you can't call these "soft" drinks) were loaded with two surprises: cocaine and caffeine. The two main types of beverages were Colas and Olas. History finds that the Colas win out, as we no longer have any Olas being sold.

Coca-Cola was created in 1886 and sold as a patent medicine for 5 cents a bottle. Other manufacturers tried to break in on the success that Coca-Cola was enjoying. The copycats were attempting to one-up our champion by increasing the amount of cocaine and caffeine in their products.

From the president's Home Commission, the Bureau of Chemistry in 1907, reports that the following sodas contained cocaine and caffeine: Afri Cola, Ala Cola, Cafe Cola, Carre Cola, Chera Cola, Coca Beta, Coca-Cola, Pilsbury's Coke, Cola Coke, Cream Cola, Four Kola, Kola Phos, Hayo Kola, Heck's Cola, Koca Nola, Koke, Kola Ade, Kola Kola, Kola Phos, Koloko, Kos Kola, Lime Cola, Mellow Nip, Rocola, Standard Cola, Toka Tona, Vim-O, French Wine of Cola, Celery Ola, Chan Ola, Kaye Ola, Lime Ola, Nerv Ola, Revive Ola, Wise Ola, Tokola.

Oh, and one simply called Dope.

In the song The Overseas Stomp (often referred to as the Lindbergh Hop) we see verse 3, line 1:
"she asked me for a bottle of Kaye Ola
I said, "Momma let me play it on your Victrola."

Kaye Ola was manufactured by A.W. Kaye of Meridian, Mississippi. It contained both extract of coca leaf (cocaine) and caffeine, which enhanced the cocaine, causing it to spike rather than come on slowly. Kaye Ola was the power drink of its day. Preferably enjoyed while sitting.

The following products still consumed today are listed in the order of appearance in the marketplace.

Root Beer was invented in1876

Dr. Pepper was invented in 1885

Coca-Cola was invented in 1886 (sold as a patent medicine – 5 cents per bottle)

Pepsi-Cola was invented in 1898 (best of the copycats)

Note: It was the Coca-Cola company that changed the image of Santa Clause from a skinny woodland elf dressed in green, to a fat man wearing the Coca-Cola colors, first seen drinking a bottle of Coke in an ad campaign.

COCA-COLA
SYRUP ⚬ AND ⚬ EXTRACT.

For Soda Water and other Carbonated Beverages.

This "INTELLECTUAL BEVERAGE" and TEMPERANCE DRINK contains the valuable TONIC and NERVE STIMULANT properties of the Coca plant and Cola (or Kola) nuts, and makes not only a delicious, exhilarating, refreshing and invigorating Beverage, (dispensed from the soda water fountain or in other carbonated beverages), but a valuable Brain Tonic, and a cure for all nervous affections — SICK HEAD-ACHE, NEURALGIA, HYSTERIA, MELANCHOLY, &c.

The peculiar flavor of COCA-COLA delights every palate; it is dispensed from the soda fountain in same manner as any of the fruit syrups.

J. S. Pemberton,
Chemist,
Sole Proprietor, Atlanta, Ga.

CHAPTER TWELVE:
GRAMOPHONE OR VICTROLA

The phonograph or record player, was invented in 1877 by Thomas Edison. The original record was made on a cylinder wrapped with tin-foil and did not last long. These phonographs were costly to create, with little or no profit, and Edison moved on to invent the light bulb, leaving the recording project for others to develop.

But because this was not an electrical appliance, but operated by hand-winding the coil spring inside, it could be used anywhere. The music of an orchestra could be enjoyed within your gazebo, in your private home, or place of business. Such luxury and wonderful freedom had never been imagined.

Prior to 1894 all recordings were on round cylinders; once they went into commercial production the playing surface was made out of wax. The cylinders easily tracked accurately because their diameter remained the same from one end to the other, but they could only play for two minutes, they were very bulky to store, and wore out quickly.

They were also costly to produce.

Emile Berliner was born in Germany in 1851 and made his home in the United States. At the turn of the century, he initiated the large scale transition from phonograph cylinders to disc records. Working with the same concept, he invented the Gramophone in 1888. It was commercially launched in the early 1890s. He owned the Gramophone companies of the United States, Germany, England and Canada.

The discs were read from the outer edge to the smaller center which necessitated the gramophone speeding up as the recording progressed in order to maintain play-back speed. As the years passed, additional improvements were made to the drive system and sound reproduction. The record discs were longer playing and stored very compactly in comparison to the cylinder, but the kicker was that they were much cheaper to produce while selling for an equal price. Soon the cylinder would be an experiment gone wrong, to be completely replaced by the disc.

The name Gramophone eventually became shortened in everyday vocabulary to Grammy and this is what is referred to when we see the Grammy Awards.

In September 1906, Eldridge Johnson, the owner of The Victor Talking Machine Company began selling a record player he called "Victrola", and they became so popular that the term Victrola started being used to describe any phonograph player. The turntable and amplifying horn were tucked away inside of a wooden cabinet. This was not for sound quality but purely for visual esthetics; a phonograph player that looked like a piece of furniture. The sound from the Gramophone came out through a horn, whereas the Victrola's horn was hidden.

Below: Thomas Edison

**Below: The Gramophone and the Edison Wax Cylinder Phonograph
(note: both utilize external horns for sound projection)**

**Below: One of the world's greatest vocalists, Enrico Caruso, stands in
contemplation of the sound from a Victrola phonograph.**

Long playing 10-inch discs were introduced in 1901. These were called "Concert Grands". Two years later the 12-inch deluxe records hit the market. By 1909, only the 12-inch records were produced, and this was the beginning of what was to become the 78 rpm period. All records prior to 1904 were recorded on one side only with the other side left completely blank. They were about a ¼ inch thick and were very hard (shellac) with no flexibility whatsoever and would crumble like a cookie if struck, although some records were made out of either celluloid or hard rubber. All recordings were mono with low fidelity which did not see improvement until 1925.

The two-sided record was patented in June 1904 by Colin C. McKenzie of Whitehorse, Yukon, Canada, who had simply attached two records back to back. Because of such conflict between recording companies, a U.S. court ruled the double sided record to be common property. The jump from 78 rpm records to long play 12 inch 33 ½ rpm records marks the move to vinyl; a more flexible, shatter–proof and thinner product that increased the longevity of each individual record. Vinyl discs remained popular until the 1980s.

CHAPTER THIRTEEN: TIN PAN ALLEY

The songwriters, publishers, and arrangers who dominated the American popular music market in the late 19th and early 20th centuries set up shop in New York in an area of the city that became known as Tin Pan Alley. It was located in the block of West 28th Street, between Fifth and Sixth Avenues in Manhattan.

Tin Pan Alley began in 1885 when a group of music publishers moved into the same district of Manhattan. It flourished until the 1930s when the radio and phonograph were out-grossing sheet music sales.

How Tin Pan Alley got its name has always been in debate. There is a newspaper article from the period that describes all the pianos playing at the same time, at different tempos, auditioning or rehearsing different songs, to sound like someone beating tin pans in an alley. Many credit this first mention of a tin pan alley to the newspaper article, whereas others claim to have personally come up with the name. Whatever its origins, it was adopted and came to represent the beginning of the U.S. music industry.

In its prime, Tin Pan Alley was a thriving mall of activity with music writers, vaudevillians, Broadway producers, musicians, and song pluggers (these were pianists, singers, and performers who made their living demonstrating songs to promote the sale of sheet music) running in and out of the offices of publishers, agents, and promoters. The four and five story high buildings were entirely occupied by the music industry.

A group of Tin Pan Alley music houses formed the "Music Publishers Association of the United States" on June 11, 1895 and unsuccessfully lobbied the federal government to improve the copyright laws regarding the music industry. With undefined copyright laws (they didn't even cover melody) you could reproduce someone else's song with only a few changes.

Songwriters would often sell their songs outright for a flat fee, allowing the publisher to put any name they wanted down as composer. This title of "songwriter" could be sold to an upcoming artist to legitimize and strengthen their position in the eyes of the public and the industry: this value in a promotional aspect rivaled being the artist of a hit song. Some publishers would insist on being named as co-writer to reduce the amount of publishing percentage that was to be paid to the actual writer or the "new owner of the song".

It was double-dealing and outright scamming that drove composers like Irving Berlin to open their own publishing companies to avoid the drama. Harry Warren also opened his publishing company for the same reasons and was to create so many songs in the 1930s that he is credited for the creation of the 1930s sound.

Below: Irving Berlin

When a hit song was produced in Tin Pan Alley, smalltime vaudeville performers would pay for the rights to perform the song, however, big time vaudevillians were given first choice to premiere predicted hits for free because their performances promoted the sheet music sales.

George Gershwin was an American who had been born in Russia. He was a songwriter and composer who created compositions in both classical and popular styles. In the 1920s and 30s he produced classics like "Rhapsody in Blue", "An American in Paris", and "Porgy and Bess". He got his start in Tin Pan Alley as a song-plugger, earning $15 a week. He published his first song in 1916 at the age of 17: his total earnings for the song was 50 cents. In 1919, he wrote "Swanee" and was heard singing it at a party. The next thing he knew, Al Jolson was taking it to Broadway and Gershwin's career soared.

The American Society of Composers, Authors, and Publishers (ASCAP) was founded in 1914 to aid and protect the interests of established publishers and composers. New members were admitted to this exclusive society by sponsorship from existing members only.

During WW2 the United States federal government felt that the far reaching influence that music had on the American public could be used to increase the patriotic mood of the nation. The government contracted the writers in Tin Pan Alley to produce war songs that would inspire the U.S. citizens and the troops in the field.

By the way, today most songwriters perform their own music. This was motivated by record producers so they would only have one person (who was usually desperate for a recording contract) to deal with, thus making it easier to extract a larger percentage of profit which could come out of song royalties. Prior to that, there was commonly a songwriter – who, in many cases, had no performing skills and spent all his time honing his or her craft as a writer - and a stage performer, who had spent all their time developing a strong stage personality and delivery. Putting these two together gave you the strongest end product. But when it came to finances, the recording company would rather have only one person on payroll.

The correspondence between money and art is a mischievous one.

Below: George Gershwin

CHAPTER FOURTEEN: THE GILDED AGE

The Gilded Age comprises a thirty year span and includes the elegant eighties, the gay nineties and the first ten years of the 20th century. Much was to take place during the Gilded Age. During this time, one of the most popular trends was to produce songs performed as a dirge. A dirge is simply a style of delivery when presenting lyrics to an audience. It means, roughly, to sing with emotion and lament. The tempo was unimportant; it was the intent and content that mattered. We often think of the funeral dirge when the subject is brought up, but that is only because the misery of the funeral march was a very perfect place for the emotional dirge. But much - though not all - of the popular music of the age was played in dirge style, and would be referred to as tear-jerkers today.

During the gay nineties one of the best ways for an entertainer to make money was to sell his or her sheet music. This was before the radio or television, and before phonographs became widely available at an affordable price. Silent films had little impact during this period on the music and entertainment industry. There was good money in vaudeville but, if you weren't a world acclaimed star, the big money was more likely to be made in sheet music sales. If your skill lay in song writing, sheet music was your ticket to success because every household parlour had a piano and the family would enjoy singing and playing together. These social skills had to be developed. Men sang, ladies played the pianoforte, or piano, as we say today. This was also an important part of courtship; these talents provided an elevated status socially.

The piano, at this time, was considered a ladies instrument and the sale of sheet music was a profitable one. If you wanted to sell sheet music, you needed to cater to the Victorian lady. This customer was overly virtuous, would rather die than commit scandal, and wore so much clothing that you could only glimpse her head and occasionally her hands. The popular song with these ladies was the emotional, heart-felt dirge. These somber compositions were a gold mine for the publishers of the day, and were performed not only in the family parlour, but gained their popularity in

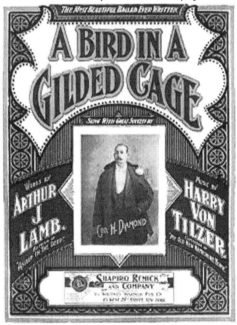

minstrel shows, mining camps, saloons, vaude, burley and med shows, and the traveling theatrical companies touring the countryside. This is the music that would eventually be pushed out by ragtime during the last decade of the Gilded Age.

CHAPTER FIFTEEN: THE PEDDLING CRAZE

During the Gilded Age, North Americans developed a craze for physical activity. One popular form of entertainment was bicycling, and it became a passion that seized the country in the late 1800s. Prior to this, the first bicycle was called the Velocipede by its creator. However, most people referred to it as the "bone shaker" because of its uncomfortable ride. This was the result of a wrought iron frame and wooden wheels encased by tires made of steel. The pedals were attached directly to the front wheel and, despite the uncomfortable ride on the rough roads and pathways of town, they became so popular that they were ridden inside of buildings, much like roller-skating rinks and clubs. Cycling teams were even formed. The Velocipede was replaced by the penny-farthing or high-wheel bicycle. The large front wheel and small rear wheel looked like a penny and a farthing coin side-by-side, hence the name. The large front wheel enabled faster speeds since the bicycle was direct drive.

Below: The Penny-farthing

**Below: The Penny-farthing was
difficult to mount and to stop without practice.**

In the 1880s the invention of the "safety bicycle" or "diamond bicycle" and "step-through bicycle" (which we now call just the bicycle) could have wheels of the same size, although often one was a bit larger than the other. One big selling point was that the rider could reach the ground with their feet while mounted which provided a feeling of safety. By peddling a chain and sprocket driven rear wheel, these bicycles had a lower center of gravity and were less likely to do a header. The penny-farthing was notorious for sending its rider over the handlebars.

During this time there were sales of dicycles which had one or two seats side-by-side and two wheels, also side-by-side. The wheels were larger than the seats and passengers rode between the two big wheels. There were, of course, unicycles and tricycles and, additionally, there were quadracycles (four wheels that were pedaled like a pedal-car). All were developed between 1817 and 1880.

Below: The Otto-dicycle

Below: Both riders are steering simultaneously, and both sets of pedals power the rear wheel. Only the woman has the bell. Only the man has the brake. What can we conclude from this?

Below: This dicycle is technically a quadracycle, having four wheels.

Both men and women were part of the bicycle mania of the 1890s. Women were great targets for this business because bicycling gave them a taste of freedom they had not previously experienced. More casual, loose fitting clothes were designed for women to ride in, and manufactures profited not only from bicycle sales, but clothing and accessory sales as well.

Daisy, Daisy,
Give me your answer do!
I'm half crazy,
All for the love of you!
It won't be a stylish marriage,
I can't afford a carriage,
But you'll look sweet, upon the seat
Of a bicycle built for two !
(1892)

**Below: The tandem bicycle
"...a bicycle built for two"**

CHAPTER SIXTEEN: SILENT MOVIES

In the beginning there were no "silent movies", there were only "movies". It was not until long after the invention of the movie soundtrack that these early movies earned the title of *silent* movies.

If you have learned anything about me so far, it should be that I am likely to skip the details about all the people who spent their lives in the development of the film process and move right on to the information that I personally find interesting. You are right, so here we go.

Although it was always the intention right from the start, the challenges in creating synchronized dialogue was not made possible with an acceptable level of integrity until 1926. Silent movies are films made prior to that time, that had no recorded sound and, particularly, no spoken dialogue. The actors would communicate through muted gestures, mime, and title cards.

The great era of "Silents" fascinated audiences from approximately 1894 to 1929. Because silent films were mute, onscreen intertitles, later referred to as simply titles, were used to narrate story points, contribute key dialogue, and sometimes even comment on the action. The "title writer" became a key professional in silent film and was often different from the author who had created the story. Titles often became graphic elements themselves, featuring illustrations that enhanced the action or were text augmented by the artistic Victorian flourish designs of the day.

In the early days of silent film, live music was there right from the beginning. A pianist or organist was always on hand to guide the audience through the emotional passages of the film, building excitement, creating the energy of the great chase, lightening the mood for a frolic or comedic scene, assisting the flow of tears, building suspense, announcing the hero or villain, and provoking a smile or frown. Some movie theatres were equipped with an instrument called the Mighty Wurlitzer which could simulate some orchestral sounds along with a number of percussion effects such as bass drums and cymbals. Additionally, it could produce sound effects ranging from galloping horses to rolling thunder. At the height of the silent movie era, movies were the largest source of employment for instrumental musicians.

Below: The Mighty Wurlitzer

Percussion was to become important in many movie houses and the performer would also be skilled in the art of Foley. A Foley artist contributes sound effects in perfect timing, creating a more exciting and believable experience for the movie watcher. They would reproduce the sounds of a door creaking, footsteps, dogs howling, roosters crowing, glass breaking, thunder, screams, and even the yawn of a waking child. The technique was developed by Jack Foley (1891-1967).

During the age of "talkies", Foley artist were brought in during post production to enhance sound effects that were not loud enough or descriptive enough, or sometimes simply hadn't been picked up in the original recording, yet were necessary. Dramatic radio shows also relied on Foley.

Below: An early Foley artist (the man second from right) adding effects to a live radio play in the 1920s.
He is holding an effects board with which he can simulate ringing telephones and closing doors.

Silent film stars exaggerated their movements and facial expressions to further emphasize and communicate thought and emotion on the film stage. Many were basically transferring their live stage skills to the movie stage. Later, some actresses began using subtlety in their facial expressions and stage movements, and acquired a larger fan base for the effort, as the screen affords a more intimate relationship with an audience.

Because there was a lack of colour in film, toning or tinting was sometimes used. A scene dipped in a blue tint depicted night, when dipped in yellow or amber it was to suggest daytime. Green represented the mysterious and red was used to make fire more obvious. Sepia toning was a common and popular look that produced a warm image. Some films were hand tinted at the cost of time and great expense.

Thomas Edison, who invented the phonograph and the light bulb, also produced the motion picture camera in 1889 and, although this section is not about him, I should mention, he invented over eleven hundred other useful items: busy, busy, busy.

Mack Sennett, a Canadian-American, heard there was money in motion pictures. In 1909 he signed up with W. D. Griffith Productions and was soon making 5 dollars a day. Griffith was known as, "The Father of Film" and was one of the true great pioneers of the motion picture business.

Once Mack Sennett knew his way around a studio lot he began developing revolutionary ideas as to how comedy should be created. He opened his own movie studio and was soon out grossing everyone else in the industry. He was the innovator of slapstick and was crowned "King of Comedy". In 1912, he founded Keystone Studios in Edendale, California. The main building was the first totally enclosed film-stage and studio in history. Mack put movies on the map and introduced us to Laurel and Hardy, Charlie Chaplin, Harold Lloyd, The Keystone Kops, Mabel Normand, Ford Sterling, Ben Turpin, Roscoe "Fatty" Arbuckle, Harry "Bing" Crosby, Chester Conklin, Gloria Swanson, Marie Dressler, Teddy the Wonder Dog, Wallace Berry, Harry Langdon, and Al St. John. Mack Sennett himself, was already a celebrity actor and had starred in over four hundred movies: eleven of them as Sherlock Holmes. His career had begun in burlesque, and he had developed as a writer, producer, actor, singer, dancer and comic genius providing the world with ever lasting memories.

Below: Mack Sennett

The Keystone Kops, Mack Sennett's creation, were so funny and so famous that police departments all over North America altered their uniforms to include military styled officers' caps to change their image to look less like the Keystone Kops.

Below: the outrageously funny Keystone Kops.

Sennett's Bathing Beauties were so popular as to inspire the cover girl/pin-up image, enhancing advertising and giving way to huge postcard and poster sales. Other Sennett stars, Charlie Chaplin and Harold Lloyd moved on to start their own movie studios: unbelievable amounts of talent moved through the doors of the Keystone studio lot.

Below: Mack Sennett's Bathing Beauties.

Below: Stars of the silver screen:
top left to right: Louise Brooks, Rudolph Valentino,
bottom left to right: Stan Jefferson (Stan Laurel) and Buster Keaton.

Below: top left to right: Harold Lloyd, William S. Hart, bottom left to right: Mabel Normand, and Oliver Hardy.

**Below: top left to right: Gloria Swanson, Greta Garbo
bottom left to right: Lillian Gish, Charlie Chaplin**

The introduction of "talkies", which happened simultaneously with the onslaught of the Great Depression, meant the end of the silent movie era and was devastating to live music performers. Some of the major instrument companies also suffered and went out of business when silent movies came to an end.

There were many other contributors to the earliest of films and wonderful examples of historic documentation into which I urge my readers to explore. Toward the end of the book I will share titles of books that you will enjoy from authors who deliver intriguing information in an entertaining manner. Broaden your knowledge concerning the world of show business: the early pioneers gave us so very much and just being aware allows you the opportunity to doff your hat and whisper, thanks.

CHAPTER SEVENTEEN: THE TALKIES

1926 the three lads at Warner Brothers had financially put their lives on the line. They had spent over two million dollars on the process of adding sound to movies and gambled that the public would go crazy for the idea. Part of the stress they were feeling came from the fact that they didn't have two million dollars, and it was sink or swim. If the talkies were a success in the trial theatre it would mean that, in order to play them, every other theatre would need to install special camera equipment that included amplifiers and a full speaker array. To convince the industry to make this change the talkies would need to be very impressive.

They sat in the back of the theatre with a full audience awaiting the experimental preview of the first talky. It was August 6, 1926: within an hour they would either be declared as amazing innovators or dismissed as nitwits. As the movie opened, a man on screen stepped forward and began to introduce the movie. He was talking and the audience both saw and heard him! When he finished the introduction, the audience applauded loudly and enthusiastically en masse. The answer had been given. The Warner Brothers had created history and magic: the industry would never be the same. As the film progressed, the New York Philharmonic Orchestra played on screen and the audience watched as each musician performed, and the sound, note for note, was heard as the startled audience watched the perfect synchronization of sound and picture.

There had been sound in movies as early as 1921 but these had always been shorts, not full-length movies, and only had instrumental scores, not dialogue. The breakthrough was not realized to its fullest until Warner Brothers released the debut of "The Jazz Singer" in 1927, starring Al Jolson, who had already earned the title of "World's Greatest Entertainer". He performed scenes in blackface in the movie and sang six songs ensuring the success of this talkie with the star power he had developed over the years. The audience was sold. The idea of being able to go into a theatre in a remote town to see and hear Al Jolson singing would sell any movie concept. The industry jumped into talkies, the floodgate opened, and silent movies began circling the drain.

**Below: The Jazz Singer – the movie that sold
the talkies to the public.**

**Below: Star of "The Jazz Singer" Asa Yoelson, a New York Jew.
He changed his name to Al Jolson.**

Below: Al without his traditional blackface makeup.

CHAPTER EIGHTEEN: JUG BANDS

Early jug bands were typically made up of African-American vaudeville and medicine show musicians, with a sprinkling of White minstrel show musicians and, of course, anyone with an inclination to make music. In the late 1800s and during the early turn of the century, musical instruments had to be made by hand. Because of their expense, citizens who lived paycheque to paycheque found it difficult to purchase new instruments for their children. The impact of the assembly-line created by the Ford Motor Company had not yet influenced all of the musical instrument builders of the day. There were few music stores with rows of pre-made instruments for sale. Families and individuals who wanted to play music, but couldn't finance an instrument, would take it upon themselves to build their own. Often a substitution seemed adequate. An example would be the percussive sound produced when striking or scraping a washboard with thimbles on your fingers, or perhaps the fact that blowing into a jug - in just the right way - could produce a tuba-like sound. It was common in the early days to make a banjo or mandolin out of a gourd, metal pie tin, or bread pan, and a discarded guitar neck or a broom handle. Some guitars were even fashioned from cigar boxes. Oh the ingenuity was well displayed and the craziness that it produced made it all the more fun! So fun, in fact, that established musicians were often seen playing in these bands, adding the sound of their very legitimate and expensive instruments to the mix.

Somewhere in Louisville, Kentucky, around 1905, an inspired and, indubitably, drunken instrumentalist raised his just-emptied whiskey jug to his lips and, picking up the beat of the string band he was accompanying, started blowing. The deep belly of resonance he created was simultaneously dramatic, comedic, danceable, and tuba-like! From out of this emerged the magnificent jug bands.

Below: Terry Devine, referenced by Wikipedia as one of the best jug players living today. He resides in Greater Vancouver, B.C.

A jug band is a band employing a jug player (although some wave this rule) and a mix of traditional and homemade instruments. The traditional instruments would most likely be the banjo, guitar, mandolin, violin, ukulele, tenor guitar, harmonica, kazoo, and the occasional brass or reed instrument. The homemade substituted instruments are usually a washboard, jug, washtub bass (or gutbucket), stovepipe, comb-and-tissue-paper/kazoo, or spoons. This just goes to show the creativity of people determined to play music.

The jug band community provided an entire additional market of musicians who were attempting to unravel the mysteries of jass and blues: their contributions were enormous. Are they ever mentioned in jazz books by jazz critics? No. Never. (Someone's vexed). Jazz critics turn up their nose to jug bands, spasm bands, washboard bands, juke bands and gutbucket bands because they only want to talk about what they think you, the reader knows about. That seems to be legendary jazzers like Louis Armstrong, Duke Ellington, Charlie Parker and Miles Davis. I have asked myself for years why these "experts" in jazz never look to the roots. They display every musician who was great like they woke up, found an expensive instrument under their beds, and started playing immediately at a level of expertise that set them apart from the rest of the musical community. Are you kidding me? Many of the players were born into poverty and played on the streets in jug bands before even realizing they were gifted. Without that opportunity they might have never hefted a musical instrument and the world would have been at the loss. So let's talk about them.

It was sometime in the early 1900s that jug bands first sprang up in Louisville, Kentucky. These bands were playing the music influenced by ragtime, that would be called jazz, and as the concept spread we began to hear jug bands in Memphis, only they were playing in a style that was eventually to be known as the blues. Today, the guitar is associated with the blues, but that instrument's dominance is actually a rather recent development beginning soon after the start of the 20th century. During the 19th century, it was the fiddle, the banjo, and the kazoo that were the dominant blues instruments for both White and Black North American musicians. Having not yet gained the formal title of blues, it was then referred to as country-western music, folk music, or even Black music.

Jug bands played on the Mississippi and Ohio River paddlewheel boats, and played at the Kentucky Derby in the early years. They were in vaudeville, on the streets, in southern nightclubs, and playing parties and socials. Who were these musicians playing in these "novelty" bands? Well, how about Louis Armstrong: he was in **Jimmy Bertrand's Washboard Wizards**, and so was Johnny Dodds. **The Seven Gallon Jug Band** had Clarence Williams, and when Clarence had the **Clarence Williams Washboard Five**, King Oliver was playing cornet in the band. Later Clarence developed the **Clarence Williams Jug Band** with Clarence on jug and Willie "The Lion" Smith on piano, Lonnie Johnson on guitar, and Albert Nickels on clarinet. By the way, Clarence Williams, the jug band pioneer, was the first to use the word jazz in the lyrics of a song.

**Below: The Masters of Jazz who loved to play in jug bands.
Top left to right: Louis Armstrong, Willie "The Lion" Smith
Bottom left to right: Joe "King" Oliver, Clarence Williams**

Being in these jug bands was not a decision made to increase their wealth, although many were quite successful. These bands played because it was crazy fun and a real joy to produce the art that is music. But oh! **The Mound City Blue Blowers**, the first band to ever record a kazoo, was such a huge hit that everybody wanted to play in that jug band and it went through some players that were to become big names such as: Eddie

Condon, Jimmy Dorsey, Gene Krupa, Eddie Lang, Red McKenzie, Jack Teagarden, Frankie Trumbauer, Muggsy Spanier, Glen Miller, and Dick Slevin.

The Louisville Jug Band, also called **The Dixieland Jug Blowers** made their first recording in 1926 in Chicago. Recording opportunities were very scarce at this time, but soon bands like **The Memphis Jug Band** would do over one hundred recordings which were labeled as "race records" and sometimes "country" although the music was commonly blues or jazz.

Below: The Memphis Jug Band

By the late 1920s the new sounds of innovative jug bands dominated the American pop-music scene in such areas as Birmingham, Alabama, Cincinnati, and Brooklyn. **The Five Harmaniacs**, an eccentric quartet led by Sid "Red" Newman on banjo and harmonica was among the first acts to ever record using a jug. And although the four members of **The Five Harmaniacs** were White vaudevillians from New York and North Carolina, the group's recordings were listed in the "race market" section of record-company catalogs. In 1926, they wrote and recorded their two most memorable hits "Coney Island Washboard Roundelay" and "Sadie Green, the Vamp of New Orleans".

It wasn't long before the jug novelty had significantly infiltrated the jazz and country music scenes. **The Cumberland Ridge Runners** was a white string ensemble that featured future country luminaries Karl and Harty, and Doc Hopkins: they used an earthen jug to produce their bass rhythms. **Ezra Buzzington's Rustic Revelers** stylized jazz and country with their strings, clarinet, and jug in pop recordings such as "Little Brown Jug." **Kentuckian Earl McDonald's Louisville Jug Band** became renowned for its performances in 1903 at Churchill Downs during Kentucky Derby week, a spotlight gig that became a tradition. The Kentucky Derby featured a jug band every year right up to 1930.

In 1913, McDonald hired a teenager named Clifford Hayes to play fiddle with his band. Within a year the **Louisville Jug Band** was attracting huge crowds in New York City and that led to a successful two-year stand in Chicago. After McDonald caught Hayes with his fingers in the till, Hayes left and started his own group. The men reunited, however, as part of the **Dixieland Jug Blowers** which was assembled for two extraordinary studio recording sessions in 1926 and '27: "Love Blues," "Hey! I Am Blue," and "Everybody Wants My Tootelum" were remarkable pieces of recording session history.

Below: Ballard Chefs Jug Band from the late 1920s through the 30s. Sponsored by The Ballard and Ballard Flour Company, they gained a huge following that included many radio shows appearances.

The **Dixieland Jug Blowers**, with Earl McDonald, sported a horn section with Johnny Dodds, one of the greatest clarinet players of the 1920s. Johnny also had **The Johnny Dodds Washboard Band** with his brother, Baby Dodds, on washboard. Baby Dodds was Gene Krupa's tutor on stick technique and it was Dodds who invented the kick drum. Modern Drummer magazine refers to Baby Dodds as the father of jazz drumming. The washboard player who invented jazz drumming: another interesting jug band contribution.

In Tennessee, Will Shade's legendary, down-and-dirty **Memphis Jug Band** was kicking up dirt in live stage and street performances that were to spread their name and fame. **The Picaninny Jug Band** in 1932, had Will Shade on harmonica.

The stage presence and delivery of travelling medicine shows influenced the **Memphis Jug Band**. The group initially employed comedian Charlie Polk as its long-standing jug blower. With musicians Furry Lewis, Will Weldon, Tee Wee Blackman, Charlie Burse, Ben Ramey, Vol Stevens, and Jab Jones, the **Memphis Jug Band** gave us songs like, "The Old Folks Started It", "Beale Street Mess Around", and "Stealin' Stealin' " , the latter covered by Jerry Garcia and David Grisman on the record album Shady Grove, released in 1996. The **Memphis Jug Band** was closely rivaled by **The Cannon's Jug Stompers**, whose signature hit "Minglewood Blues" was covered by Jerry Garcia in **The Grateful Dead**. Gus Cannon's band additionally released "Walk Right In", "Going to Germany", "Bring It with You When You Come", "Mule Get Up in the Alley", and "Viola Lee Blues".

Below: Gus Cannon's Jug Stompers

There was **Tampa Red's Jug Band and Hokum Band**, and Bo Carter's popular **Mississippi Sheiks**, who were all becoming extremely well-known. **Fred Ozark's Jug Blowers** (1924) featured Cliff Edwards "Ukulele Ike" who was later the voice of Disney's Jiminy Cricket and sang, "When You Wish upon a Star", one of the world's most beloved songs.

Below: Cliff Edwards "Ukulele Ike"

The kazoo was invented by a man named Alabama Vest in 1840 for people who couldn't tolerate the tickling feeling one got from playing the comb-and-tissue-paper. It was originally called the membranophone, was patented January 9, 1883, and renamed the kazoo. The modern submarine shape was created and patented in 1902. It was finally commercially produced in 1916 and went into mass production in New York by the Original American Kazoo Company. The company is still located in Eden, New York and is still producing kazoos with the original equipment it used in 1916.

The first recording of the kazoo was by Dick Slevin in **The Mound City Blue Blowers**, which also featured Red McKenzie on comb-and-tissue-paper. It was Red who was on the recording of "Crazy Blues" in 1921 by **The Original Dixieland Jass Band**. Red McKenzie also took advantage of his comb-and-tissue-paper and kazoo skills while playing in the **Paul Whiteman Orchestra**. Paul Whiteman was known as the "King of Jazz". **The Mills Brothers** started as a four-piece kazoo/barbershop quartet, with John Jr. on ukulele and eventually guitar. King Oliver (justly named "King" of New Orleans jazz) performed often with two kazooist in his band. He was the man who trained and nurtured Louis Armstrong. By the way Louis Armstrong also performed with kazoo players. Audiences loved the kazoo.

Jug Bands Inspire Rock and Roll

In the late 1950s and 1960s there was a jug band revival in the United States headed by bands Like the Orange Blossom Jug Five, featuring Dave Van Ronk; the Jim Kweskin Jug Band; the Even Dozen Jug Band; The Nitty Gritty Dirt Band; and many others.

Rock critic Ed Ward once listed the most important bands of the early 1960s as the Rolling Stones, the Beatles, the Byrds, and the Jim Kweskin Jug Band (below).

The same music was experiencing a revival in Europe, minus the jug and with a tea-chest bass instead of a washtub bass: the Europeans called it "skiffle". The word skiffle originated in Chicago in the 1920s, meaning "rent party". A rent party was a house party with a novelty band and a nominal entrance fee. The hope was to raise enough money to get the landlord off their back for another month!

Skiffle music was extremely popular in Europe, and the man who was credited as the "King of Skiffle" was Lonnie Donegan. He was born in Glasgow, Scotland on April 29, 1931 and influenced British musicians more than anyone before him. Lonnie was a vocalist, songwriter, and musician and was the most successful and influential recording artist before the Beatles. He had thirty-one Top 30 U.K. hits.

Below: Lonnie Donegan, singer, guitar and banjo player

Jug band and skiffle music influenced the development of rock & roll as in the following examples: **The Even Dozen Jug Band** featured John Sebastion and Steve Katz. John later formed **The Lovin' Spoonful** and Steve Katz became a member of **Blood, Sweat and Tears**. Maria Muldaur was in **The Even Dozen Jug Band** and the **Jim Kweskin Jug Band** and later enjoyed a solo career as a blues/jazz and country artist.

The **Mugwamps Jug Band** gave us Zal Yanovsky of **The Lovin' Spoonful**, also, Cass Elliot and Denny Dougherty who both went on to become famous in **The Mommas and the Papas**. **The Nitty Gritty Dirt Band** - a jug band up to 1967 – became **The Dirt Band**. **Mother McCree's Jug Champions** featured Jerry Garcia: that band became **The Grateful Dead**. **The Instant Action Jug Band** became **Country Joe and The Fish**.

In Europe, **The Midnight Special Skiffle Band** (UK) had Irish lead singer Van Morrison, and he was also in the **Sputniks Skiffle Band**. Mick Jagger was in the **Kingston's Bucktown Skiffle Group**. Cliff Richards was singing in the **Dick Teague Skiffle Group**. Folk musicians Martin Carthy, John Renbourn and Ashley Hutchings, and rock musicians Roger Daltrey, Jimmy Page, Ritchie Blackmore, Robin Trower, David Gilmour, and 11 year old David Bowie, and popular beat music successes Graham Nash and Allan Clarke of **The Hollies**, were all in Skiffle bands. Ringo Star was in the **Eddie Clayton Skiffle Group** at the same time John Lennon was forming **The Quarrymen Skiffle Band** with Paul and George which eventually became **The Beatles**!

Below: the author's band "The Genuine Jug Band"
From left: Tony McBride on percussion, Douglas Fraser on tenor guitar and vocals, guest Jack Stafford on saxophone, and Terry Devine, gut-bucket bass.

CHAPTER NINETEEN: THE BLUES

The first blues song published was in 1908 by Antonio Maggio and entitled "I Got The Blues". It was also the first published song to use the word blues. The next song to be published was Hart Wand's "Delta Blues" in 1912. But the credit for popularizing the blues went to Mr. Handy.

William Christopher Handy called himself W. C. Handy and he was born in Alabama on November 16, 1873 and left us on March 28, 1958. W.C. was a cornet soloist and bandmaster with minstrel shows. An educated man, he received his musical degree in 1892, and went on to teach music at the Alabama Agricultural and Mechanical College for Negroes.

Below: William Christopher Handy, age 19.

Now the story I have come across through the years from several sources was that W.C. had his jazz band playing at a highfalutin' social gathering for a prominent White political leader. It was about 1905 and he was delighted to get this gig and was being paid very well. During a break he received a request to play "his native music". Confused, he inquired as to what was wanted. In response they asked if he wouldn't mind if a local group of musicians come up and perform a couple of tunes. Since it didn't affect his pay, and elongated his break time, he graciously agreed to let them play. Entering the stage area, and carrying homemade instruments, a three piece jug band began to play the music that one day would be associated with the blues, and the crowd started throwing money up onto the stage. W. C Handy smiled as he watched until the amount of money on the floor exceeded what his band was getting paid for playing the whole day. His interest was now ignited concerning this music and he set off across the country listening, learning, questioning, and playing this musical style which he would come to label "the blues". There are additional stories about W.C. Handy, and several towns, like Tutwiler for instance, all lay claim to Mr. Handy having invented the blues there. But as I mentioned, he toured the Mississippi Delta, looking and listening.

In 1909, W. C. Handy wrote a campaign song titled "Mr. Crump". Edward Crump won the campaign for mayor and Handy latter reworked the song and it became "The Memphis Blues". Publishing this song, which was the first example of twelve bar blues to be published, we see William becoming known as "The Father of the Blues" in 1912. Having not yet established sound business techniques, he unfortunately sold the rights to "The Memphis Blues" for one hundred dollars. After it became the enormous hit that it was to become, he realized his mistake. The Memphis Blues is said to have influenced the creation and popularity of the foxtrot.

W. C. Handy educated himself in regards to the publishing business and opened a publishing company with partner, Harry Pace. In 1914 he wrote one of the most famous blues songs entitled "The St. Louis Blues". He also wrote "Yellow Dog Blues" the same year and "Beale Street Blues" in 1916. He went on to compose dozens of songs and write two books. W. C. performed the first blues concert in New York City's Carnegie Hall in 1928.

Below: The first recording by an African-American singer was Mamie Smith's 1920 rendition of Perry Bradford's "Crazy Blues".

Understand that the Black community had been singing and playing what we now call the blues for eighty years or so before it was published and legitimized as a musical style. At that time it was known casually as Southern slave music. It was enjoyed often in juke joints, which were places where Blacks went to listen to music, dance, or gamble after a hard day's work. Juke joints were usually the social room on a working plantation and date back to the early 1800s.

In 1912, W.C. Handy made the "Southern slave music" popular: he published it, he labeled it "the Blues", and he brought it to light in the form of twelve-bar. This made it commercial, allowing local musicians to define it and recreate it easily, as it could be played using just three chords. The formula for twelve-bar blues mirrors the call-and-response scheme commonly found in African and African-American music. The blues can be played in different formats, but it was the twelve-bar blues with its catchy 4 bar vocal, 4 bar repeat of the same vocal, and 4 bar vocal answer that caught on.

Example:
I heard that my baby, was seein' another man,
I heard that my baby, was seein' another man,
I went to see that fellow, with my razor in my hand. – D.E.F.

Now don't let yourself be fooled by copyrights. The early laws governing copyright were very flexible and often didn't cover melody. Before the copyright laws were enforced, songs written, to which no one was making a claim, were considered ripe for the picking. An example would be that Hughie Cannon (who legitimately wrote "Won't You Come Home Bill Bailey") filed for copyright in 1904 and made claim to be the author of the song "Frankie and Johnny". History proves that this song had been sung in 1863 after the Siege of Vicksburg during the American Civil War. I found references to it as far back as 1830 in which a shooting took place involving a woman named Frances (alas the victim of the dreadful moniker: Frankie) who shot her boyfriend Johnny over an alleged affair with Nellie Bly. Her execution followed, and the song appeared thereafter.

As for the origin of the term "the Blues", I saw an old African-American woman from south Mississippi explaining it on a documentary. She said that back in those days they would say that there were spirits they called the "blue devils" that could make bad things happen or make people unhappy. When someone was down and out, or sad or upset, they would say, "Lord, he gots a bad case of the blue devils," or "the blue devils must've got in ta him!" In reading on the internet, I found that in the late 1700s and early 1800s slaves often thought that people coming to America from England brought the "low" spirits (no doubt...being sold into slavery is such a buzz kill). These spirits were believed to be able to cause problems for people and make them feel bad. Washington Irving in 1807 wrote of a man "under the influence of a whole legion of the blues", and a young Ulysses S. Grant wrote in 1846, "I came back to my tent, and to drive away the blues, I took up some of your old letters". So over time, people began to use the term "blues" or "blue devils" to explain or describe the same thing that we still call "having the blues" today.

Here are some of the blues greats:
• Tommy Johnson (1896 - 1956) recorded the blues from 1928 to 1930. Being an alcoholic surely shortened his life, but he had an advanced guitar style that influenced many a Delta blues man.
• Blind Lemon Jefferson (1897 - 1929) Born blind, he taught himself how to play the guitar and was considered "the Father of Texas Blues". In the 1920s he was a very sought after performer. He recorded over one hundred songs.
• Tampa Red (1904 - 1981) This man was called "the Guitar Wizard" in

the 1920s and 30s. He was born in Georgia and his real name was Hudson Whitaker, but he grew up in Florida and had bright red hair. His slide guitar technique and admiration for the outrageous helped him gain fame in the band called **The Hokum Boys** with a hit song called "It's Tight Like That".

• Leadbelly (1888 – 1949) was born in Louisiana by the name of Huddie Ledbetter. He had hits like "Rock Island Line", "Goodnight Irene", and "Midnight Special".

• Robert Johnson, (1911 – 1938) pictured below, is one of the greatest blues men to have lived, producing great songs like "Sweet Home Chicago", "Love in Vain", "Cross road Blues", and "Kind Hearted Woman". These blues standards are considered must-learns by most bluesmen.

• Son House (1902 – 1988) set the Mississippi Delta ablaze in the 1920s and 30s. He would often mix gospel and the blues.

• Bessie Smith (1894 – 1937), the most famous female singer of the 1920s. Bessie was referred to as "The Empress of the Blues". She enjoyed tremendous amounts of record sales.

• Charley Patton (1887 – 1934). In the 1920s Charley influenced some of the greatest blues men of our times. He was a first class star and was constantly in demand with a successful career.

There are four styles of blues:

*The term Piedmont blues, also known as East Coast blues, refers to a guitar style. It is a stride style of guitar picking.

*The Delta blues is one of the earliest styles of blues music. It originated in the Mississippi Delta. Guitar, harmonica, and cigar box guitar became the dominant instruments used. The original instrumentation for blues bands was fiddle, banjo, and kazoo.

*The Chicago blues is a form of blues music that developed in Chicago, Illinois by taking the basic acoustic guitar and harmonica-based Delta blues and adding electrically amplified guitar, amplified bass guitar, drums, piano, and sometimes saxophone, and making the harmonica louder by using a microphone and an instrument amplifier.

*Jump blues is an up-tempo blues usually played by small groups and featuring horns. It was very popular in the 1940s.

The blues is a purely African-American musical form. It has derived from obscure and mostly undocumented origins to become the most extensively recorded and influential of all types of folk music. This is the music that makes you wipe a tear from your eye and conjures up images of smoky honkytonks, desolate saloons, and Memphis street corners. The blues was not recorded until the 1920s and those recordings established the blues as one of the most popular music forms of the day. Blues music was the harmonic foundation for jazz, and later it was the emotional inspiration for rock 'n' roll.

In the 1950s rock 'n' roll was to lean heavily on the blues during its development, and two successful performers, Jerry Lee Lewis and Elvis Presley, introduced the blues as rock 'n' roll and put it - and themselves - on the map.

Below: legendary blues vocalist, Billie Holiday.

CHAPTER TWENTY: JASS AND JAZZ

The music was first called jass and retained that label for a few years before it was changed to jazz. Here is the story that I have always liked (though there are several other theories):

The band to first gain recognition for playing this new music came up from New Orleans, having just toured the South. The all White band members of the **Original Dixieland Jass Band** were an overnight sensation. Most everyone, and especially the young folks, could talk of little else. The year was 1917 and there were more mature folks that didn't care for this new music, claiming it was in cahoots with the devil. In a coordinated effort to eliminate it, they took cans of white-wash, big brushes and defaced the billboards and posters by white-washing the J from the word Jass. Well, as you can see, what we were left with was unacceptable, and it was splashed all over town. The city officials agreed: something had to be done. Either the band had to leave town, or the name had to be changed.

There are two theories as to the origin of the word jazz being chosen to replace jass. Some people claim that, in retaliation to the "morality police squad" defacing their billboards, the band went with "Jazz" because it was a word commonly used since 1912 on the West Coast, where it had a low sexual connotation meaning "to fornicate". It was an inside joke to the band: the laugh would eventually have come full circle when the band was to play San Francisco. On the West Coast, where jazz meant intercourse, jazbo or jazbeau meant lover of the ladies and a jazz baby was an easy woman.

Another theory involves a clarinet player who had become a bit of a legend. His name was Jazbo Brown. At this time the best money to be made for a Black musician was playing in a Creole band. The Creole bands consisted of educated men able to read music; it was a prerequisite to performing with them. Jazbo was unable to read music. He would listen to the band performing the night before his audition and memorize every song, note for note, having heard them only this once. With the sheet music placed in front of him, he even memorized when to turn the page. He would be hired and he continued the bluff for nine years before being found out. At that time, the other players realized what a genius he was and word spread. His nick-name happened to be Jazz. Some people claim the music was named after him.

The early jass music took form in New Orleans around 1895, and combined elements of ragtime, marching band music, Scottish folk songs, Irish jigs, German waltzes, French quadrilles, blues and African polyrhythms. These polyrhythms were different beats played at the same time, often syncopated and accented. Africa also brought us polyphonic melodies: the combination of several simultaneously-played melodies.

There were musicians intentionally playing as novelty bands, incorporating zany humour, costuming and props. As jazz was unlabeled in the early years, the lack of definition caused many bands to be referred to as novelty bands and/or spasm bands. Prior to 1917, bands that were calling themselves jass bands were playing a form of evolved ragtime that was later to be called jazz.

With very few exceptions, jazzy-ragtime style music before 1917 was in 2/4 time; popular music after 1917 was in 4/4 time and was called jazz or fox-trot. Many pieces of music published in New Orleans in 1915, or 1916, in 2/4 time were re-published in 1917, in 4/4 time.

In 1915, Joe Frisco (a vaudeville dancer and comic) brought the **Dixieland Five Jass Band** to Chicago to play Lamb's Cafe. Tom Brown was the trombonist and band leader and Joe Frisco booked them in as **"Brown's New Orleans's Jass Band"**. They were so well liked that Al

Capone had his photograph taken with the band. Although they were a massive hit in town, jass had to wait two more years before a recording would give it world recognition and commercial acceptance.

The origins of **The Original Dixieland Jass Band** tell an interesting story: they started out with Johnny Stein as band leader and drummer. In those days they were called **Johnny Stein's Dixieland Jass Band**. The band spent many months traveling through the Southern States absorbing the varied styles of the local musicians. They were encouraged and influenced by the developments created by predecessors like Jelly Roll Morton (1890-1941), Stalebread Lacombe (1885-1946), Buddy Bolden (1877-1931) and Freddie Keppard (1889-1933). They now felt ready to return to their hometown of Chicago; the object was to sell the idea of "Jass" to a white marketplace.

They returned with two bookings set up in the Chicago area. However, the first gig was at a hotel, and when they arrived they found that it had been recently closed down. This meant a two week lay-over with no financial income to support them. Trouble was brewing. Then a telegram arrived informing them that they had an opportunity to play at Reisenweber's Cafe on Columbus Circle and 58th Street, Manhattan, a fashionable restaurant and night-spot. They had the endorsement of Al Jolson, the highest paid entertainer of the day. Jolson had seen them, loved them, and put in a good word about them.

The band was excited until Johnny Stein said, "Listen guys, it's a great break, but we have a contract signed to play in a few weeks and we can't break the contract." Then the band said, "Wrong. *You* have a contract signed: *you* have to play the gig. We are going to Reisenweber's Cafe." They left Johnny Stein holding the bag. They grabbed a new drummer and called themselves **The Original Dixieland Jass Band**, played Reisenweber's and, because of the popularity of the foxtrot, they performed most of their songs in 4/4 time instead of the traditional 2/4 like ragtime. That difference created the Dixieland sound.

Below: Johnny Stein's Dixieland Jass Band. Johnny on drums.

In the twelve days before his contracted gig would commence, Johnny Stein put a new band together with Jimmy Durante as the piano player. But, back at Reisenweber's Cafe, the new band leader, Nick LaRocca had the **Original Dixieland Jass Band** in the right place at the right time. The band created quite a stir and Columbia Records rushed in to record them only weeks after they had arrived in the city. The very first recording was the "Darktown Strutter's Ball" recorded at The Columbia Gramophone Company on January 30, 1917. It was not released first, however. A decision was made to hold it and record a second song "Livery Stable Blues". As the quality of the first recording at the Columbia Gramophone Company was deemed as substandard, the second song was recorded at the Victor Talking Machine Company and on February 26, 1917 "Livery Stable Blues" was recorded and subsequently released. It sold a million copies. The **ODJB** became a national overnight sensation.

The **Original Dixieland Jass Band** claimed to have invented jass. The first claim was a bit tongue-in-cheek, but the press ate it up and so they delivered the claim straight-faced, as if hundreds of black bands had not been playing jass years before. The fact is they were the first band to record jass commercially, and the first band to establish jass (later jazz) as a musical idiom or genre.

On February 8, 2006 the **ODJB** was inducted into the Grammy Hall of Fame for their 1917 recording of "Darktown Strutter's Ball". It was the first jazz Recording, first jazz standard, and most popular jazz song of all time. The man who wrote the "Darktown Strutter's Ball" was Canadian Sheldon Brooks, a song and dance man, who went on to write the song that made Sophie Tucker famous called "Some of These Days".

There are many magic moments in the development of jazz, some after the **ODJB**, some before. Some musicologists think that ragtime is jazz. Others think that the blues is not a separate category of music, but is merely a style of jazz. They stand firm to that opinion ignoring the proof that the blues was being played for decades before ragtime or jazz had surfaced. Still others think that jazz originated with the Louis Armstrong-Earl Hines recordings in the late-mid 1920s, and that everything before that is "funny-hat" music. With so many opinions, nothing will ever be settled. However, the **ODJB** were pivotal for the time.

Scat singing is a jazz vocal technique in which the singer substitutes improvised nonsense syllables for the words of a song, in attempt to sound and phrase similar to an instrument. The first person to ever scat sing was from Vicksburg, Mississippi. The year was 1902 and his name was Joe Simms, an old comedian. So copying Joe, Tony Jackson and Jelly Roll Morton, and several others grabbed it and used it. This was long before Louis Armstrong and Cab Calloway became known for scat singing.

Below: Jelly Roll Morton, third from the left, with other performers. (1917)

The term Dixieland is generally used for jazz which is played in a quasi-New Orleans style by White musicians. Here is the origin of the word Dixieland: During the American Civil War, the Bank of New Orleans provided currency for the Confederate States of America. It issued a ten dollar bill with the word "dix" written on the back, which was French for "ten". That bill became known as a "Dixie". Hence, the idea of the South being Dixie-land. The term has nothing to do with the Mason-Dixon Line.

Jazz

When jass became jazz the music was already at full momentum. The change in terminology happened in Chicago late in 1917. Jazz spread across the country and into Europe, infecting the public as no other music before it had done.

In North America jazz was king and, although the **Original Dixieland Jazz Band** had kicked it off, they were soon to be left behind by the surfacing jazz bands that just needed to have the ice broken for them. Now that jazz was an accepted commodity, the marketplace was open and the money was being dished out to acts that could deliver. Larger bands appeared like the **California Ramblers** in the early 1920s, a nine-piece that could play most anything and with a heavy flocculation of band members (always great), their sound changed and was consistently innovative. This band had players like Red Nichols, who had been influenced by Bix Beiderbecke, but was a better overall musician and a far better sight reader than Bix. Also in the **California Ramblers** were Jimmy and Tommy Dorsey, Miff Mole, Adrian Rollini and, through the years, 63 other musicians. When you hired the **California Ramblers**, you would likely not get exactly the same band you last saw: they were always changing, but always great. They also formed a smaller group called **The Goofus Five**.

So many great jazz bands were to form, perform live, and record that they cannot all be listed and I am only mentioning my personal favorites. Since I mentioned Red Nichols you need to know that as a cornet/trumpet player, he was one of the very best, and he recorded in over four thousand sessions in the 1920s alone. He apparently worked more than anyone else during that era. Bix Beiderbecke was a cornetist, pianist and composer and was featured in the Jean Goldkette, **Paul Whiteman Orchestra**, and **The Wolverines**. In 1924 Bix was replaced in **The Wolverines** by Jimmy McPartland. Singers like Al Jolson, Eddie Cantor, and Fanny Brice were singing jazz in Broadway musicals.

There are those who point to the sessions with Louis Armstrong and Earl Hines as the greatest moments in jazz history. These are truly recordings that need to be listened to.

Cliff Edwards, Helen Cane, Rudy Vallee, Gene Austin, Ruth Edding, Ted Lewis, Josephine Baker, Ethel Waters, and so many others were belting out jazz tunes on the radio and on records.

Great bands like **George Olson's Orchestra, The Coon Sanders Nighthawks, Harry Reser's Band,** the **Firehouse Five, Arkansas Travelers, Red and Miff's Stompers, King Oliver's Creole Jazz Band, Original Memphis Five, Waring's Pennsylvanians, Earl Hines Band, Louis Armstrong and His Hot Five, The New Orleans Rhythm Kings, Clarence Williams Band, Frankie Trumbauer's Band,** and **Kid Ory's Band**: each of them created some of the greatest music in existence.

"If you have to ask what jazz is, you will never know."
-Louis Armstrong

**Below: The Wolverines Jazz Band featuring
Bix Beiderbecke on cornet (fifth from left) 1924.**

When you hear reference to Creole bands, know that this refers to the musicians' heritage, and not the musical style they perform. Creole means someone who is native born, however, in Louisiana it is often commonly used to describe Blacks with French or Spanish blood. In old Louisiana, prior to the Louisiana purchase, all you had to have was a drop of this mixed blood and, if you could prove it, you were treated like a White man even if you did not look it. Creoles were often free people of colour who were typically financially stable and were pillars of their community. Louisiana was first settled by the French, sold to the Spanish, and eventually purchased by the colonies. Its European outlook towards its Black and mixed Black population was unlike any other part of North America.

CHAPTER TWENTY ONE: HILLBILLY BANDS

Coined in 1925, hillbilly music was once the label for what is now known as country music. The term is still used today to refer to old-time music or bluegrass. The term hillbilly boogie was finally changed in the '50s to rockabilly and is a common terminology.

In a 1900 New York Journal article, they defined hillbilly: "a Hill-Billie is a free and untrammeled white citizen of Alabama, who lives in the hills, has no means to speak of, dresses as he can, talks as he pleases, drinks whiskey when he gets it, and fires off his revolver as the fancy takes him."

Performers involved with country-western music wanted to distance themselves from the hillbilly image.

It was a constant struggle to record a country song and not be labeled as a race record or hillbilly tune. Problem being that many recording artists at the time were actual hillbillies, such as Cliff Carlisle (who was really recording blues songs). Other early artists were Ernest V. Stoneman, Riley Puckett, Don Richardson, Uncle Dave Macon, Al Hopkins, Jimmie Rodgers, the Carter Family, Hank Snow, Charlie Poole, the North Carolina Ramblers, and The Skillet Lickers.

Below: Jimmie Rodgers, Charlie Poole and the North Carolina Ramblers, and Riley Puckett.

In the '20s, barn-dance shows were featured on the radio, and country music soared in popularity. The most important thing to happen was the "Grand Ole Opry" which aired first in 1925 and is still going today.

Below: Ryman Auditorium. Built in 1892, it was to become the most beloved of all the venues that housed the Grand Ole Opry.

In the '30s and '40s cowboy songs and "the singing cowboy" was all the rage, with big stars like Gene Autry, The Sons of the Pioneers, and Roy Rogers and Dale Evans recording phonographs, appearing on radio shows and in movies. We also had other cowgirls like Patsy Montana (no relation to Hannah) with her hit song, "I Want to Be a Cowboy's Sweetheart".

Below: Entertainers in music, radio, movies, and T.V.
On left: Dale Evans, Roy Rogers, and Trigger.
On right: Gene Autry

Bob Wills would produce country swing and was the first country artist to add an electric guitar to the band in 1938. Bob appeared in Western movies and so did Spade Cooley and Tex Williams. We were later to have country boogie artists like Tennessee Ernie Ford. In the '50s Bob Wills and His Texas Playboys gave us Texas swing and honky-tonk music.

Below: Bob Wills

Below: Bob Wills and His Texas Playboys tour bus

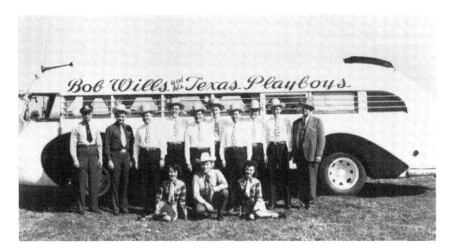

CHAPTER TWENTY TWO: AUTOMOBILES

For the touring performer, the luxury of owning an automobile was a God-send. Finally the artist was no longer at the mercy of the baggage handler who was at fault for both broken musical instruments and missing musical instruments. Suitcases and trunks could be moved safely and, for theatrical companies, trucks provided access to towns and communities not serviced by the railroad, enlarging the marketplace and increasing profits. Freedom came in the shape of the automobile.

The Ford Motor Company was established in 1901. Henry Ford's creation of the assembly line was to bring about the North American industrial revolution; prior to that, the United States and Canada were farming nations. What children call summer vacation, which equates to three months away from school, was originally created so that they would be home to bring in the harvest.

The world was changing and, as the industrial revolution was to affect the production of so many products, the pace of life was to quicken. The more stress on the average citizen, the more they would need a release from that stress, and that meant...entertainment!

More work, and a way to get to it, was a win-win. People from outlying towns who had cars could now attend theatrical performances and vaudeville shows that they would have missed without motorized transportation. Life was speeding up!

The Ford Model T, known as the Tin Lizzie and Flivver, was an automobile produced by Henry Ford's Ford Motor Company from 1908 through 1927. The Model T made 1908 the historic year that the automobile came into popular usage. It is generally regarded as the first affordable automobile, the car that "put America on wheels". Some of this was because of Ford's innovations including assembly line production, instead of individual handcrafting.

Below: Ford Model T car...

... and the truck

Henry Ford wanted every American to be able to afford and enjoy the automobile. When he was able to reduce the cost of production, he also reduced the retail price, retaining only the same ratio of profit for his company. The Model T cost $850. in 1909 and, as assembly line techniques improved, the price dropped to $440. in 1915. By the 1920s the price had dropped again to $300., and in 1924 it was $290. Henry had let middle class

America in on automobile fun. Businessmen of that calibre no longer exist today. By 1914 every other car purchased was a Ford.

While still a major purchase, the fun of the new automobile was customizing it and making it your own. Purchasing dusters (riding cloths), goggles, cloth tops, picnic baskets, running boards, trunks and rumble seats would make your new car stand out from everyone else's, even though they only came stock in black. The Model Ts were very slow, but the roads were so terrible that ten to twenty miles an hour was all you could want. There will always be the discontented, and for those there was the expensive Pierce Arrow and the Panhards that would do fifty miles per hour. In 1906, Frank Marriot drove a steam powered car on Daytona Beach called the "Stanley Steamer" to a speed of 127 MPH.

1914 saw the need to install traffic lights to slow down the drivers and control the flow of city traffic. Cleveland was the first city to get them working. A speed limit of between 10 and 20 MPH was enforced in town. In 1911 the Indianapolis 500 got its start with a winner clocking in at 74 MPH.

Here is an example of personal lore: I heard this story from my father when I was a child. In the early days, while Henry Ford was just starting up his business, he was a bit strapped for money and took a loan from a neighbour and friend, for which in turn he promised 10% of the Ford Motor Company. The neighbour was left with only a dinner napkin describing the transaction signed by Henry Ford.

Years later, in the mid 1930s, the old man arrived at the Ford Motor Company asking to speak to Henry and, after explaining his business, was taken in to meet Edsel, Henry Ford's son who was now the CEO of the company. Mr. Ford asked him what his business was and the old man replied by just laying the napkin down on Edsel's desk.

In those days, 10% of the company would have broken them. It represented an enormous amount of cash that simply wasn't available to be shelled out and Mr. Ford, recognizing the signature of his father, knew he was looking at the real thing.

"What do you want?" was all he could say. The old man replied, "My grandson would like a new Ford Car."

Looking up, Edsel said, "And you would trade this for a new car?"

"It would make him very happy," the old man replied.

"Tell you what... we will send him a new Ford automobile every year of his life, till the day he dies, in exchange for this napkin and your word that we are settled."

That's how it turned out, and both parties were very happy with the results.

CHAPTER TWENTY THREE:
NIGHTCLUBS AND SUPPER CLUBS

In North America, nightclubs first began to appear in the early 20th century. These venues sold alcohol (sometimes illegally) and promoted entertainment in the form of live music and song (jazz and swing was popular in the 1920s and 1930s); dancing girls often performing burlesque routines; and various other small stage performers including magicians, freak shows, and comedy, which were often vaudeville performers still scrambling for work after the demise of vaudeville houses.

During the Volstead Act era, United States citizens were not allowed to consume or possess alcoholic beverages from the year 1919 to 1933. At this time Canadian cities, like Montreal, were to become host and hostess to millions of Americans who needed a night out. The legal drinking age was (and is) 18 years, and clubs stayed open until 3:00 A.M. which was later than American night spots stayed open. In the '20s they seldom closed their doors; booze and money flowed like water. Canadian distilleries made a fortune during that period. Additionally, cases of Canadian booze were smuggled into the U.S. and the producers still brag about it in today's modern advertising. Montréal already enjoyed a sophisticated and slightly naughty reputation as the Paris of North America, which added to the allure.

In the U.S., prohibition roadhouses evolved into supper clubs which became popular in the 1930s, providing a place to enjoy high-end cuisine while watching a stage show with well known personalities and, at this time, while enjoying an illegal beverage. Prohibition was very good for the entertainment business.

New York's Cotton Club, which operated during the prohibition era, was a Whites-only club. This was a rule that was strictly enforced, although the entertainment was peppered with the very best of Black performers including Cab Calloway, Nat King Cole, The Nicholas Brothers, Lena Horn, Count Basie, Fletcher Henderson, Duke Ellington, Fats Waller, Louis Armstrong, Billie Holiday, Bessie Smith, Ella Fitzgerald, and Ethel Waters. The clientele consisted of major stars like Al Jolson, Jimmy Durante, George Gershwin, Eddie Cantor, Fanny Brice, Sophie Tucker, Mae West, Judy Garland, and Irving Berlin.

Below: The Cotton Club in the district of Harlem, Manhattan, New York. The club operated from 1923 to 1940.

Following the repeal of the Volstead Act, supper clubs continued to flourish in the '40s and '50s, as popular social entertainment hot-spots. They died out in the 1970s. Nightclubs have evolved and lived on, though only some still utilize the talents of live performance. Today many nightclubs have DJs, canned music, and televisions. These stand as a lost marketplace for the live entertainment industry which, musically, is teetering on its pirated heels.

CHAPTER TWENTY FOUR: RAGTIME

Ragtime was the first truly official American music genre. Peak popularity for ragtime was between 1897 and 1918. It began as dance music in the red-light districts. Ernest Hogan was an innovator and key pioneer who helped develop the musical genre, and is credited with coining the term ragtime.

It is now generally conceded that early piano ragtime developed as an imitative art: imitative in that the piano was used to exploit earlier banjo techniques to the full – one piano being able to reproduce the effect of two, three, or even four banjos. This banjo effect may be noticed in some of the reconstructions of early ragtime. But truly, ragtime and the piano were meant to be together and I don't think the piano has felt better since.

The earliest published rag located is entitled "New Coon in Town", composed by Gunnar, and published "for piano" by S. Brainard's and Sons of New York and Chicago in the year 1884. It is sub-titled "Banjo Imitation." However, prior to that there is said to have been hundreds of raggy tunes being played.

Coon songs were written and published between 1880 and 1920, and in the mid 1890s were outrageously popular, both here and in Britain. They were written in the popular ragtime style of the day and, for awhile, it seemed that every songwriter put their pen to one. It was both White and Black artists that were churning out these tunes, all of which were written as humorous songs, but at the same time, each one was disparagingly racist and stereotypically damaging to the Black community. After the turn of the century, the public were recognizing them as racist, and the fad had run its course.

Below: examples of popular sheet music advertising "Ragtime Coon Songs".

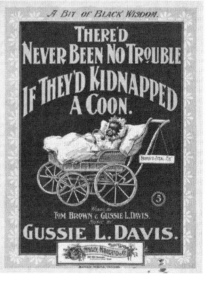

A man from Sedalia, Missouri named Scott Joplin is credited by many to have finally created the definitive style that defines ragtime music; he wrote some of the finest rags ever produced. However, many of the other performers who had written ragtime could not read or write music and came to Scott Joplin to have their songs written down. When doing so, often the agreement was that Scott Joplin was the only name to be put on the sheet music and, although they may have received payment, they received no credit for writing the tunes. Between 1898 and 1916 he was apparently responsible for some fifty ragtime compositions.

Below: Mr. Scott Joplin "The King of Ragtime".

Jelly Roll Morton's comment was that Scott Joplin "lacked the chops" to play many of the songs he claimed to write. Scott Joplin, eventually diagnosed as insane, stuttering and suffering from memory loss, died of syphilis on April 1, 1917. That was the year his precious ragtime was to fall from favour to be replaced by the coming of jazz.

A ragtime piano player, who also played jazz and popular music, was composer, lyricist, and dignified showman, Eubie Blake. He was the first Black man to appear on stage and perform without wearing blackface. He died in 1983 at the age of ninety-six (although he claimed to be one hundred). No matter how old Eubie got he could still play piano like he was a teenager. He once told me he started smoking heavily when he was five years old, and never had stopped. It seemed like nothing could take this man from us. He was gifted with enormous hands - he called them "spider hands" - that could span the keyboard of the piano, reaching notes that other players simply could not. He would write songs that sometimes encompassed those notes so that he would be the only one who could play them. He was the last of the original great ragtime men.

In January 1897, an alderman, Sidney Story, proposed a city ruling for the city of New Orleans to permit the establishment of a section of the French Quarter of the city where prostitutes and madams would be able to conduct business. While it was never legalized, it was understood that it was given "permission" to operate as such. It was called Storyville: a 38 square block area. The district's main avenue was Basin Street. There were even two Storyvilles: Uptown side "Back O' Town" (West of Canal Street) which was for Blacks; and the downtown side, (East of Canal Street) was for Whites. In those days a brothel prostitute was known as a "Jazz Belle", while her customer was a "Jazz Beau" or "Jazbo".

Below: A Storyville Jazz Belle enjoying a glass of rye.

As ragtime music developed in New Orleans - by the soon to be great players like Jelly Roll Morton, Buddy Bolden, and King Oliver - we find banjo players, piano, and horns players and, often, five-piece bands performing in Storyville. Prior to labeling this music as ragtime, these bands were referred to as spasm bands.

Storyville was closed down by the government in 1917. This, coincidentally, was the same year jazz surfaced and was recognized as a popular music.

A most wonderful man was the poet Robert W. Service who lived from 1875 to 1958. He was a British citizen, a bank clerk and resident in the Yukon, Canada, who wrote poems about life in the North. He, in fact, mentions ragtime in one of his most famous poems, "The Shooting of Dan McGrew". In the opening stanzas, he sets the scene of the poem in the Malamute saloon, where a "kid" is playing ragtime on the piano:

> *A bunch of the boys were whooping it up in the Malamute saloon;*
> *The kid that handles the music-box was hitting a jag-time tune;*
> *Back of the bar, in a solo game, sat Dangerous Dan McGrew,*
> *And watching his luck was his light-o'-love, the lady that's known as Lou.*

> *When out of the night, which was fifty below, and into the din and the glare,*
> *There stumbled a miner fresh from the creeks, dog-dirty, and loaded for bear.*
> *He looked like a man with a foot in the grave and scarcely the strength of a louse,*
> *Yet he tilted a poke of dust on the bar, and he called for drinks for the house.*
> *There was none could place the stranger's face, though we searched ourselves for a clue;*
> *But we drank his health, and the last to drink was Dangerous Dan McGrew.*

> *His eyes went rubbering round the room, and he seemed in a kind of daze,*
> *Till at last that old piano fell in the way of his wandering gaze.*
> *The ragtime kid was having a drink; there was no one else on the stool,*
> *So the stranger stumbles across the room, and flops down there like a fool.*
> *In a buckskin shirt that was glazed with dirt he sat, and I saw him sway;*
> *Then he clutched the keys with his talon hands — my God! but that man could play.*

CHAPTER TWENTY FIVE:
THE CIRCUS CAME TO TOWN

Step right up!

The documented information concerning circuses is extremely scarce and misleading. Most of the circus history available to the public has been provided by overzealous and imaginative circus press agents, with information repeated from one to the other, occasionally with embellishment. "Facts" have been supplied by Hollywood screenwriters, popular fiction writers, and journalists who put little to no time into investigating their sources. One of the misconceptions is that the circus dates back to Roman antiquity. The Roman circus was actually the fetus of what would become the modern racehorse track, the common denominator being the word circus which means "circle".

The circus was a creation of England, and was primarily concerned in its early conception with horsemanship, but it also included jugglers, tightrope walkers, and clowns. But European circuses are not our subject.

North American Circuses

Now we are getting somewhere. Around 1835, a traveling menagerie of exotic animals - which included an African elephant - was touring the New York area. Traveling light and fast with the use of canvas tents, this undertaking proved to be very successful. This enterprise was under the guidance of a group of businessmen (instead of being controlled by bickering circus families) and was the beginning of the American circus.

Below: P.T. Barnum and General Tom Thumb, a fully grown adult.

In 1871 Phineas Taylor Barnum, known as P.T. Barnum, created the P.T. Barnum Menagerie and Circus with his business partner, William Cameron Coup. P.T. created an exhibition referred to as "the museum of human oddities" which contained things like a flea circus, a loom run by a dog, the trunk of a tree under which Jesus' disciples sat, a hat worn by Ulysses S. Grant, Ned the learned seal, the Fiji Mermaid (a mummified monkey's torso with a fish's tail), midgets, and Chang and Eng the Siamese twins. P.T. Barnum was such a colourful character that any opportunity for you to follow up by reading his life-story would be time very well used as you will find it entertaining and enlightening.

William Coup added the second ring, and then a third ring under the big top as he had the tent elongated to accommodate a larger audience. The standard size for a circus ring was forty-two feet in diameter. It was his brainchild to transport the circus by rail. His two innovations were to be copied by the whole circus industry.

James E. Cooper and James Anthony Bailey had been operating as the Cooper and Bailey Circus since the 1860s, and their show featured a baby elephant named Columbia, which they advertised as the first elephant ever born in the United States. P.T. Barnum offered to purchase this elephant as it was an enormous drawing card for the circus. Though they were unable to come to agree upon a price for the pachyderm, they did decide to combine the two shows and become the Barnum and Bailey Circus in 1881.

Five brothers with a childhood fascination for the circus changed their name from Rungeling to Ringling and eventually created the Ringling Brothers Circus. Founded in 1884, it was one of the largest and best run touring companies in North America. In 1907 they purchased the Barnum & Bailey Circus, which continued to tour separately. In 1919 they merged the two circuses to become Ringling Brothers Barnum and Bailey Circus, promoted as "The Greatest Show on Earth!".

In the early circuses, seating was only on one side of the ring, and usually reserved for ladies and children - this area was called "the box". The other side was referred to as "the pit", and was standing only, occupied by the gentlemen. When you see ads on posters referring to the "ladies' side", they mean the seating area. There is some suggestion that in 1835 circuses were traveling with bleachers, and some with fabric covered seating.

People would come into town from neighbouring farm areas and spend the day. A boon for local businesses and of course, since restaurants didn't exist, food had to be purchased at inns and saloons. Very soon the circus venders were to see the profit in selling food and drinks on-site.

Sideshows referred to the shows that were not seen under the big top. It is a contraction of the original term which was "outside shows". The first of the sideshow vendors were the whisky stands. Other vendors auctioned off clothing and novelty articles. Sale by auction was the most common exchange of merchandising and was not replaced by price ticketed articles until the advent of retail stores. Long before there was cotton candy and popcorn, they sold gingerbread, soda-pop and candy. There were, of course, also games of chance to amuse patrons of vice.

Music was a big calling-card for the circus and, as the big brass bands were very popular in the day, for the circuses a bandwagon was a symbol of success. So much associated with success, that there became a common term "jumping on the bandwagon". The brass band in the parade on opening day also performed in the big top. The bandwagon carried them through town and advertised the sound of the circus. Often there was an additional wagon featuring a gloved musician playing the steam calliope, which was also a favourite, and continued the excitement of the circus atmosphere through the streets. Around 1857, circuses started offering after show concerts which often were provided by minstrel show performers. An extra charge of between 10 cents and 25 cents was charged, and happily paid.

Below: This was the bandwagon that so many wanted to jump on.

Yet again, we see the influence the circus has had on show business in general: two circus band members, led by a man named Dan Emmett, were responsible for the creation of the minstrel show, thus changing all of show business history in North America. Benjamin Franklin Keith was working in dime museums and also with the P.T. Barnum Circus as a side show barker, and was later to join forces with Edward Franklin Albee who worked as Barnum's ticket-taker. Together they created the industry that would monopolize vaudeville in America. Oddly enough, the concept of vaudeville was conceived by Tony Pastor, who went from being a singing clown to circus ringmaster, then to theatre manager.

Entertainers from the big top provided a whirlwind of excitement. You would see jugglers, tightrope walkers, clowns, tumblers, acrobats, animal trainers, balancing acts, ventriloquists, unicycles, bullwhip artists, stilt walking, various wild animal shows, contortionists, knife throwing, fire dancing, human pyramids, hat manipulation, and the human cannonball. From the sideshow the acts that could be seen were: armless wonder, bearded lady, bed-of-nails, bee bearding, blade box, body modification, camels, chapeaugraphy (funny hat act), entomophagy (insect eating), Fiji mermaid, fire breathing, fire eating, flea circus, freak show, glass eating, glass walking, gurner (distorted facial expressions), and the half-man half-woman.

The world of the clown is one that has given us some great artists. One of the all time stars of the American circus was Emmett Leo Kelly. Born on December 9, 1898, he received his last seltzer bottle bath on March 28, 1979. He created the memorable clown figure "Weary Willie", based on the hobos of the depression era.

Below: the famous Emmett Kelly

My all time favorite clown is Lou Jacobs. He was born on January 1, 1903, and arrived from Europe twenty years later. Within weeks he had a part in an acrobatic act and was making good money ($25. a week). The next year he joined the Ringling Brothers and Barnum and Bailey Circus. He remained with them for sixty years and was the world`s most famous clown. His talent to invent comedic props, and the skill and timing to use them, was what made him into a huge star. He invented the "Midget Car". I met him in my home at one of my parents' parties as a child. He was the only circus clown that could make me really laugh.

Below: Lou Jacobs

Dan Rice was the first American clown to gain true star status. At one time his name was a household word. He had been a jockey, a strong man, singer, dancer, actor, political humourist, director, producer, animal trainer, and use to catch cannon balls on the back of his neck. He also was in politics and ran for Senate, Congress, and President of the United States, though he dropped out of each of those races. He was one of the main models for "Uncle Sam".

Early in his career, Dan only had the money for one horse at a time when horses were a main attraction at a circus. His peers made fun of him saying he had a "one horse show". Dan adopted the phrase and with that one horse, he made sure he put on a show that was fabulous. He became famous for his One Horse Show.

It was a member of Rice's troupe who, having got into a fight with a patron at the circus, and wanting backup from his friend Reuben, yelled "Hey Rube!". It has been a stand-by expression in the circus ever since.

"Hey Rube!" means: "Come help me in this fight!" It is only yelled out when a life is in danger, and every circus performer, concession worker, hawker, grinder, sideshow act, freak, and animal handler within ear shot would drop whatever they were doing and converge on the troublemaker.

We must not forget the ringmaster: "Ladies and gentlemen, boys and girls, children of all ages..." yes, you can just hear him now. His job, before stage lighting and follow-spots were invented, was to focus your attention to the next act. It was up to him to direct the performances, and make certain the pace of the show was correct. Regardless of the talent and abilities of the act, they were always described by him as the "biggest", "the most dangerous", "the most amazing" and "spectacular" performances "on the planet." He made you believe it, and his timing was impeccable. The ringmaster or ringleader was the most important element of the show.

Below: The Circus Ringmaster and the Lion Tamer had similar attire.

The geek show was typically a one person addition to the sideshow, and was often a misleading scam. It was enacted with humour so as to not leave anyone angered. An example would be a sign saying "Come See the Man Eating Chicken!" You would pay your dime and go inside to see a man sitting at a dining table eating chicken.

The "Ten-in-One" was a type of sideshow attraction that might travel with the circus, carnival, or work at the fair. This gave the customer ten acts under one tent for a single admission fee. It was often part freak show with "born freaks" like giants, midgets or people with unusual deformities. Sometimes there were "made freaks" like tattooed people, human skeletons or grotesquely obese people. But to create a variety, these shows usually included "working acts" such as a daredevil or a magician. When the show was over, there was often a "blow-off" which is an additional act offered for an additional fee. These acts were sometimes advertised as too provocative for the women folk and children, and consisted of items like pickled punks (human fetuses in glass jars of formaldehyde, usually displaying some kind of deformity. Some pickled punks were fakes made of rubber or wax), the man-to-the-gorilla routine, or the woman burned-alive trunk (she later appears uninjured).

Museum shows featured freaks - both human and animal - usually dead and stuffed, pickled, or displayed in photographs or paintings. These were "grind shows" meaning that the audience could enter at any time and look around as long as they wanted.

The "girlie shows" were most commonly called "Kooch" or "Hootchie Koochie" shows, which meant strip shows that were performed with scantily dressed dancers or, when performed "strong", involved nudity.

"Working acts" were very popular and could consist of sword-swallowing, fire-eating, fire dancing, laying on a bed-of-nails, hammering nails up your nose, self mutilation and body piercing, knife throwing, sharp shooting, and eating glass, razor blades, and goldfish (never together, as that could cause indigestion). These shows left an audience mystified and shocked. Yea folks, that's what I call show business!

Below: Typical freaks.

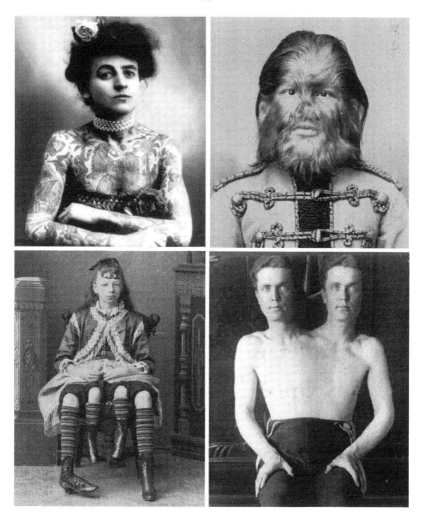

Below: Lobster Boy (notes indicate that he is 4th generation of 5 generations of "lobster people" in his family), Schlitze the pin head, and the Salon Sisters.

Below: Ella Harper, the Camel Girl (1886) is seen on this pitch card. The reverse side indicates her intentions to leave show business and "fit myself for another occupation".

My father was with The Ringling Brother's Circus as a star tumbler in the big top. He went from there to perform in vaudeville and made a lot of acquaintances. A number of celebrities would show up at his parties: Hollywood actors, directors, comedians, radio personalities, clowns, tumblers, wrestlers, singers, and, when it was off season, a car would pull up, and out would pile the freaks. Well, they were just regular people, fun and friendly. I knew Alligator Man and Monkey Girl and Frog Boy quite well. It was the early 1950s and the neighbours turned a blind eye.

Alligator Man's real name was Emmitt Bejano. He was said to be one of the most disturbing freaks of all time. As a child, I didn't find him to be anything other than interesting. I thought he was lucky to be so different. I liked his alligator skin. He was born with ichthyosis, which prevents his body from creating lipids to lubricate his skin, which caused his skin to resemble that of an alligator's. His skin wasn't his only similarity to reptiles, he shed his skin every spring and fall like a snake, and his upper eyelids couldn't move, so he blinked with lower eyelids like a lizard. When doctors examined his internal organs they found that they weren't affected by ichthyosis, though his heart and lungs were four inches lower than normal peoples. He eventually eloped with fellow circus performer Percilla Lauther, also known as "Percilla the Monkey Girl" because she was born with a thick coat of hair and a beard. Emmit and Percilla were known as the world's weirdest married couple. They were married for 57 years.

Below: Emmit's scales were subtle and don't show up in the photographs of the day.

Below: Percilla's promo picture.
(Note: her name is spelled incorrectly by the promotional staff)

During one of the parties, my Dad said, "Son, don't go out in the backyard. We have a lion tied up out there." They had been drinking with a passion, mostly because my father always supplied all the liquor, and it occurred to me to look out the window to see the lion. The lion was tied to the laundry umbrella that my mother hung the laundry on. I went to my Dad and said, "That umbrella the lion is tied too...don't you pull that out of the ground to mow the lawn?" In a panic, he and the lion tamer ran outside to fix the problem.

At yet another party, I had noticed one of the circus performers, whom I didn't previously know, had a .38 revolver in each of his rear pockets. I waited for an obvious break in conversation (children were to be seen and not heard) and asked why he had two guns. He said he trained chimpanzees and if they bit his right arm he would shoot them with his left handgun, and if they bit his left arm he had his right handgun to shoot them with. I remember thinking: life shouldn't be like that.

At a later party my Dad took me aside and said, "There have only been two blue-faced mandrill baboons ever trained in history, and we have one of them in the kitchen. Follow me." Well we entered, my dad pointed to the baboon (this was not necessary), and he started talking to his friends. The baboon, probably bored, and noticing that he was bigger than me, decided to have some fun. He backed me up against the counters and tried the old stare-down, and then he slowly bared his teeth. He had far too many teeth and his fangs were very large. I believe his plan was to scare me, and boy was it ever working out well for him. I finally broke loose when he became distracted; I left the kitchen, went to my room and sat in the dark for the rest of the night. I have never known such fear again. The event was never brought up and I never spoke to anyone about it. I personally swore to myself to never enter a baboon filled kitchen again.

Below: blue-faced mandrill, the world's largest monkey.

A year later, while traveling in my father's truck, he announced that we were going to stop off at a friend's house. As we pulled up, he turned to me to explain that his friend was the owner and trainer of Cheetah, the chimpanzee from the first Tarzan movies, and that she lived in a huge sunken pit in the middle of his living room. The pit, he said, had an iron railing around it but I could look in if I wanted. Then, just as we got out of the truck, he added, "Oh yeah, she can talk."

There was a long straight path to the front door and we walked there in silence. Dad rang the bell, we entered, and there before me was the railing. I hesitated, and the man said, "Go ahead Douglas, say hi". I walked over and peered over the railing. It was very deep; at the bottom was a heavy wooden table, a wooden chair, some toys, and an enormous chimpanzee.

Anytime the public sees a performing chimpanzee, it is always under the age of five. After the age of five great apes become juveniles and they cannot be handled without caution; their strength is ten times that of a human. Unbeknownst to the general public, full grown chimps are around five foot one or two inches tall, much larger than the babies in the movies. So she was bigger than I expected. She looked up at me. Her face was grey, but her eyes caught mine and they were powerful and frighteningly knowledgeable. I said, "Hi" and, in a slow, wheezy, drawl she huffed "Hiiiii". I ran out the door, down the path and up onto the running boards of the truck where I hung to the locked truck door for twenty minutes while my Dad concluded his visit.

We hadn't talked about it that day. I blanked it out of my mind and then began reliving it in a dream every night for about a year until I asked my Dad one day why I would have such a dream, always the same, and every night? And he said, "Because that is what happened". I then recalled the whole event, and the dreams stopped that day. Apparently Cheetah could say four or five words, and all were pronounced very breathy. I had just picked one of the words that she knew.

My mother also spent a few years with the Ringling Brothers' Circus at the same time my father was employed there. There were over one thousand employees at the circus and, as things sometimes play out, my mother and father were not to meet during those years. Mom was there because her mother could not take her with her on the road. Grandmother was a performer in Buffalo Bill's Wild West show; they had no provisions for children, but she knew the Ringling family. Out of professional courtesy, they provided room and board, and schooling for my mother.

Mother made friends with Daisy and Violet Hilton. They were beautiful girls, Siamese twins joined at the hip and buttocks, employed in the freak show. Mom went to visit them one day, but was refused entrance by their guardian, and told that they preferred seeing no one. She knew she was being lied to and so she slipped in under their tent wall for visits. They had little to no possessions and were never given much of anything other than music lessons and rehearsals to better their performance. They had been bought from their real mother in Britain when they were very young and kept as slaves to perform and appear in freak shows in the United States, for which they had seen no personal monetary compensation. They treated my mother like she was a little doll; they liked to comb her hair and listen to her stories. They were starved for entertainment and social interaction.

This is not in the history books, but it was my mother who arranged for lawyers and police to remove the Hiltons from the clutches of their keepers, gain their freedom, and to sue them for $100,000. The girls later moved on to vaudeville and did quite well.

Below: Rummaging through my mother's things, I found this photograph of Daisy and Violet (left).
The girls were later successful in vaudeville (right).

This is an isolated case and not in any way a common occurrence. The freak community was generally a very happy one. I once asked if they were ashamed of the freak show because of the occasional jeering and impolite crowds. The answer was "No, it's just theatre," they would say, "and the fact is that we make more money each year than 95% of the audience that comes in to see us. Where else could we get work? We are so lucky." It made sense, and then years later someone who thought they were being socially abused, arranged to have the freak shows made illegal. Suddenly, all the freaks were all out on the streets with no acceptance from society, no means to support themselves, and without the camaraderie of living with other freaks in a circus community.

Fortunately, the veterans had already made so much money they were able to create their own district. The town is called Gibsonton, Florida, where retired circus and carnival people can live, and the industry comes for winter vacation and conventions. It is also home of the International Independent Showmen's Association, Inc. (the Gibtown Showmen's Club).

Gibsonton has special circus zoning laws; it is one of the few places where you can keep carnival trailers and elephants on your front lawn. It was home to Percilla the Monkey Girl, the Anatomical Wonder, and the Lobster Boy. Siamese twin sisters ran a fruit stand here. At one time, it was the only post office with a counter for midgets. This is where some of the actors who played the munchkins of the Wizard of Oz movie lived.

The carnival

"Don't give them what you think they want. Give them what they want," -Patty Conklin (Conklin Shows was the largest traveling amusement corporation in North America.)

The great Patty Conklin knew how to pinpoint what was in demand, deliver it, pocket the money, and set up in the neighbouring town to repeat the process. The carnival was created to make money fast and move to the next town.

The first traveling carnival, the Canton (Ohio) Carnival Company, opened its first show in Chillicothe, Ohio, on May 30, 1899. Carnivals started up in earnest around 1902 in North America, and at that time there were 17 of them traveling from town to town. By 1937 there were 300 of them. In the early days you would sometimes find very small circuses or medicine shows attaching themselves to these new carnivals when playing the larger towns.

The carnival consisted of a midway containing games of chance and games of skill, food concessions, novelty stands, and amusement rides (which fall within the categories of kiddie rides, majors, and spectaculars). This highly lucrative business travels from fairs to events, festivals and exhibitions, each time paying a percentage of their income, or a negotiated payout, to the event organizers. In the early days, carnivals, like circuses, had freak shows, sideshows exhibiting thrill acts like fire eaters, sword swallowers and knife throwers, and sometimes burlesque (kootch shows). These shows traveled lighter than circuses did, and, with less overhead expense, could turn a profit in smaller towns and communities that the larger circus would avoid. They brought entertainment and fun.

What we call cotton candy was originally called fairy floss, and was invented in 1897 by candy makers William Morris and John C. Wharton of Nashville, Tennessee. It was introduced at the St. Louis World's Fair in 1904, and shortly thereafter, became a staple food offered at carnivals.

The Ferris wheel was introduced and invented by George W. Ferris for the 1893 World's Fair, which was held in Chicago to commemorate the 400th anniversary of Columbus's landing in America. The wheel was 250 feet across supported by two towers 140 feet high. Attached to the wheel was 36 cars (the size of buses) each fitted with revolving chairs able to carry 60 passengers. 2,160 people could ride at one time. The wheel turned on a 71 ton, 45 foot long axel. The wheel carried 38,000 passengers daily with each visitor paying fifty cents to ride. Today the largest Ferris wheel is located in Las Vegas: built in 2014 it is 551 feet tall.

**Below: A close-up of the fully enclosed cars that carried
up to 60 riders each.**

Carnivals exist in every country, and carnival rides are manufactured all over the world. Having previously owned a carnival for eighteen years, I can attest to the gratification of seeing the midway full of smiling faces, the smell of hotdogs and cotton candy, and the sound of rides spinning and carnival music playing.

CHAPTER TWENTY SIX: RADIO

The first radio broadcast in America took place on May 13, 1914, when phonograph music was relayed from Wanamaker's department store in New York to the Wanamaker's store in Philadelphia.

The first licensed radio station to open in the U.S. was in 1920 in Philadelphia. It was to broadcast to only a handful of amateur wireless operators. By late 1922, over two hundred commercial radio stations were established, broadcasting to over three million radio sets in homes throughout North America. Most sets cost from $50 to $150.

Below: a tabletop home radio.

Theatres, magazines, and live shows began losing money because of this new fad, and they began to circulate rumours that listening to the radio would damage your ears, and that electric storms started fires in homes with radios. But the audience remained entranced with the magic dial that provided entertainers from all over the country to talk to them and perform right in their living rooms for free. Record sales fell by 85%. By 1924 radio was coast to coast.

Restaurants installed radio music in place of an orchestra. Radio stations would run wires and microphones into a hotel to broadcast the hotel orchestra live. They were paying the hotel slightly more than the hotel paid the orchestra, so the hotel got free entertainment and advertising. Other hotels installed radios in the higher classed rooms.

**Below: A type of large console model
found in living rooms across North America.**

In 1925, the first amateur talent contests were run, with listeners mailing in their votes to see who would win the $25. prize. Radio, an $800,000,000. per year business in 1925, was still pleading poverty to entertainers who expected payment.

By 1927 NBC (National Broadcasting Corporation) was developed. Radio was now too competitive to get by without using headlining talent; they would have to start paying big money. The challenger was CBS (the Columbia Broadcasting Station) who approached the field with script writers reasoning that, although NBCs music show did well, nothing would hold listeners like a good story. Next we had news stories and weather reports which crushed newspaper sales.

Many of the stars of vaudeville such as Bob Hope, Edgar Bergen, George Burns and Gracie Allen, Abbott and Costello, and the Marx Brothers moved on to radio. The new medium provided variety, game shows, drama, fantasy, and music, all for free to the public. Radio secured the noose around the neck of vaudeville, kicking the chair out from underneath.

Some of the leading radio shows of the 1930s were Amos and Andy, Al Jolson Show, Fred Allen Show, Jack Benny, Burns and Allen, Dick Tracy, Bob Hope, The Shadow, Bing Crosby show, Fibber McGee and Molly, Flash Gordon, Little Orphan Annie, Reefer Madness, Texaco Star Theatre, Tarzan, The Will Rogers Show, and the Lux Radio Show.

**Below: Top L to R: Fibber McGee and Molly, Jack Benny
Bottom L to R: "Duffy's Tavern" Radio Show starring Ed Gardner,
Fred Allen, Milton Berle from "The Texaco Star Theatre".**

1929 was the year that the Pepsodent toothpaste company latched on to Amos & Andy. Two Caucasian comedians named Freeman Gosden and Charles Correll had a radio show called Sam and Henry. They had developed a following with a minstrel show type of act. They changed radio stations, but the station they left had claim to their character names of Sam and Henry. So their characters were renamed Amos Jones and Andy Brown, and the show was reborn as Amos and Andy. The Amos and Andy show became the most popular radio show of all time. So popular that, during the show, not only did telephone switchboards slow to a standstill, but factories closed early so their employees wouldn't miss the show. It was reported that there was an overall decrease in crime in North America during the time period that the show aired: even crooks couldn't pull themselves away.

Below: Gosden and Correll in blackface
Radio shows were produced in front of a live audience.

Mel Blanc was the all-time biggest talent as a voice actor, but he was also seen as a comedian with his appearances on the Jack Benny show in both the radio and television formats. Mel earned the name "The Man of a Thousand Voices".

Below: Mel Blanc, voice of radio, but best known for his character voices for Warner Bros. animations: Bugs Bunny, Daffy Duck, Porky Pig, Tweety Bird, Sylvester the Cat, Yosemite Sam, Foghorn Leghorn, Marvin the Martian, Pepé Le Pew, Speedy Gonzales, Wile E. Coyote, and the Tasmanian Devil

In the late 1970s I was talking to Mr. Orson Welles and we discussed the following event. As a young man, Orson Welles presented his version of H.G. Wells' War of the Worlds, which was broadcast on the radio through the Columbia Broadcasting System. The program narrated by Mr. Welles simulated a series of news broadcasts which brought realism to the production, suggesting that the world had been attacked by Martians, and the sound effects crew on hand made it very convincing. The fact that the show ran without commercials added to the realism. A disclaimer was issued, but only once at the beginning of the show.

Most of America was listening to the Edgar Bergen Show and, when it finished, they likely turned the dial in search for something else, consequently missing the disclaimer. It was 1937, just before WW2, and public tension was already high. Some listeners immediately called the police for verification of the alien attack and, when they didn't get any, suspiciously considered a cover up.

Orson treated the story as if it were a legitimate news report. He graphically described a Martian invasion of the United States, and the resulting destruction of major cities. Many people went into shock. Orson, however, was unaware of the realism of his performance and found out the next day when newspapers picked up the story and sensationalized it, suggesting nationwide panic had ensued. There had been no real panic, but over one thousand articles were written about the radio broadcast securing Orson Welles's name as a dramatic actor.

Below: the young Mr. Orson Welles, the narrator of War of the Worlds, and the voice of "The Shadow".

Below: Bing Crosby, Joan Burroughs (daughter of the author of Tarzan) and James Pierce who were married and worked together as the voices of "Jane and Tarzan"
Bottom: Orson Welles as "The Shadow", Gale Gordon was the radio voice of "Flash Gordon".

Charles Harold coined the terms "narrowcasting" and "broadcasting" in radio, respectively to identify transmissions destined for a single receiver - such as that on board a ship - and those transmissions destined for a general audience. It was said he had been inspired by the method of scattering seeds on a farm: a narrow toss was used to plant a row, whereas a broad sweeping cast was used to plant a field.

CHAPTER TWENTY SEVEN:
THE VOLSTEAD ACT & ALCOHOL BASED FUELS

I have included this section because, of all the things that happened in the early 20th century, the two factors that changed and challenged so much for everyone, yet, especially for the world of entertainment, was the automobile and prohibition. So here is the story you were not supposed to hear:

The Great Scheme

As we had discussed earlier, Henry Ford, by commercially producing the automobile provided mobility and transportation to the private sector and to businesses transporting goods from town to town and nationwide. Today we discuss the problems associated with the contamination of the air we breathe because of the exhaust from gas burning automobiles. Most are unaware that Ford's first cars were built to run on clean burning alcohol. Henry Ford's Model T was built with a carburetor that could switch from alcohol to gasoline. At the time, gas stations were nonexistent. Running on farm-made ethyl alcohol allowed the operator to stop at local farms (equipped with stills) to refuel his/her car during long trips through the backcountry. Gasoline had to be purchased at pharmacies.

The Standard Oil Company, and its industrialist-founder John D. Rockefeller, weren't too happy with this arrangement. After all, Rockefeller's company had a virtual monopoly on gasoline at that time. Rockefeller lobbied the government to create a law that automobiles had to be operated on gasoline. He got nowhere with it.

Since the late 1800s, there had been a growing alcohol temperance movement developing amongst reformers; it was called the anti-saloon league.

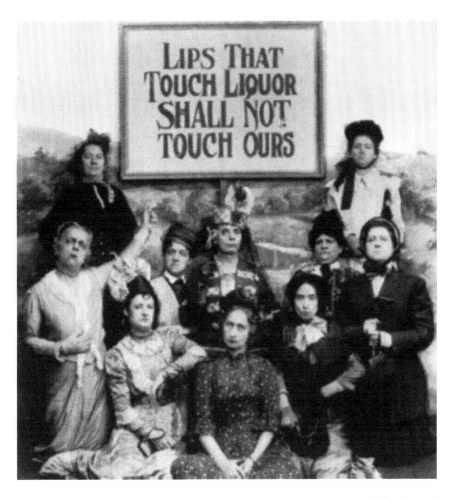

Rockefeller realized: take away *all* alcohol, and vehicles would be forced to use his gasoline. It is well-documented that local efforts to curb alcohol consumption were expanded to the national level when high-profile figures like Rockefeller joined in the anti-alcohol efforts.

Rockefeller donated $350,000. to the Anti-Saloon League (today's value would be five million dollars) which allowed the temperance movement to demonstrate on such a grand level as to force the government to pass prohibition.

Below: The feds dump hootch during prohibition.

The act was designed to:
• prohibit intoxicating beverages
• regulate the manufacture, sale, or transport of intoxicating liquor (but not consumption)
• ensure an ample supply of alcohol to promote its use in scientific research and in the development of fuel, dye, and other lawful industries and practices, such as religious rituals.

Without alcohol, gasoline was now the only option for automobile fuel, and it came to be sold at blacksmith shops, general stores, and hardware stores, in addition to pharmacies. Filling stations were soon to be deployed and the first one was in St. Louis, Missouri, while the second one opened in Seattle, Washington.

Below: 1920s era gasoline pump

Then John D. Rockefeller secretly bought up all the publishing houses and newspapers in the United States to prevent anybody exposing his involvement. Today, the lying press gets all its propaganda from the Associated Press, which is still owned by the Rockefeller family.

CHAPTER TWENTY EIGHT:
SWING, BIG BANDS AND BEBOP

Swing: Swing was a style of jazz that had been developing since bands first played it and dancers danced the Texas Tommy back in 1910 in San Francisco. Swing was being played right through the 1920s, as an underground style, popular with musicians. It was not commercially accepted until the first swing hit recording in the mid 1930s. Because musicians had been privately swinging, the bands began playing this type of music publicly the moment it became a trend. Dances included the Lindy Hop, which was the most popular. There were several different Shags being danced, and also the Balboa or Bal, which started out in San Francisco. Each city created its own style of each dance, so there were hundreds of variations.

Jazz went from "hot" to "swing" and we were to idolize groups in the late 1920s for pushing this sound and creating the popularity that would put this style on top. These were musical acts like The Paul Whiteman Orchestra, Jean Goldkette, Ted Louis, Rudy Vallee, George Olson, Harry Reser, James Last, and Fred Waring: they were the front runners and the evolution of swing was underway. The Dorsey Brothers were hits in 1928 with their first recording but swing was not to gain commercial priority until the mid 1930s. With swing we had the band following written arrangements, as these bands stepped away from the improvisation that had fueled hot jazz.

Top swing bands consisted of Harry James, Count Basie, Duke Ellington, Woody Herman, Artie Shaw, Tommy Dorsey, Benny Goodman, and Glenn Miller. Swing was to expand into dozens of definitive styles such as Texas swing, Gypsy swing, and country swing. The years of 1935 to 1946 were called the Swing Era: during that time, swing was the most popular music in North America.

Swing used more horn players than hot jazz. Gone was the tuba to be replaced by the stand-up bass, while the banjo was eliminated and guitar was brought in. Swing is not a musical form unto itself, but rather a style of jazz music.

**Below: Benny Goodman Orchestra
"The King of Swing"**

Boogie-woogie: This is piano based blues played with an eight to the bar bass line style. Most commonly this is twelve-bar blues. The dance was very smooth, but can also be done to rock 'n' roll music. Boogie-woogie thrived from 1920 to 1945. Boogie was another term meaning "house rent party".

Big Bands: In the 1940s big bands originated in the United States. They were swing bands with complex arrangements and less improvisation, fronted by crooners doing pop standards.

It was not considered a big band unless it had at least 14 to 25 musicians. The standard was a seventeen-piece band, and that is what most written arrangements were set up for. The instrumentation would consist of five saxophones, most often two altos, two tenors, and one baritone. There would be four trumpets, four trombones - which often included one bass trombone - and also a four-piece rhythm section composed of drums, acoustic bass or electric bass, piano, and guitar. However, variations to this instrument line-up are common.

Whereas hot jazz contained a considerable amount of improvisation, big band music is primarily crafted in advance by an arranger. The new sound was characterized by sweet and romantic melodies. Some of the bands on the top of the list were: Paul Whiteman, Ted Lewis, Harry Reser, Fred Waring, Leo Reisman, Abe Lyman, George Olsen, Ben Bernie, Bob Haring, Ben Selvin, Earl Burtnett, Gus Arnheim, Henry Halstead, Rudy Vallée, Jean Goldkette, Glen Gray, Isham Jones, Roger Wolfe Kahn, Sam Lanin, James Last, Vincent Lopez, Ben Pollack and Shep Fields.

Below: Big band leaders, Benny Goodman, Tommy Dorsey, and Cab Calloway.

Below: Claude Thornhill Orchestra

Below: The Paul Whiteman Orchestra

Below: The Duke Ellington Orchestra

**Below: Fletcher Henderson, one of the most
influential arrangers and band leaders in jazz history.**

The sophistication and complex harmonized melodies caused the arrangements of Don Redman's work for the Fletcher Henderson Band to make them a stand out. The flare and unique delivery proved that Cab Calloway's band would stay in the history books, and the work of Hoagy Carmichael, and later Duke Ellington, captivated millions.

Bebop and Jump Blues: The advent of World War II made it economically impossible to tour with huge orchestras. In 1948, the U.S. Musicians' Union strike made recording a record illegal till 1949. Most bands broke down to three and four pieces, and bebop emerged. Bebop is jazz, usually played with a fast tempo. This music can sound nervous, erratic, and often fragmented. This new form made way for modern jazz and contained a good deal of improvisation. Artists like Dizzy Gillespie, Charlie Parker, Bud Powell, and Thelonious Monk paved the way for so many. The new sound featured the importance of the string bass, and changed the approach to playing drums, using jagged phrasing with the bass drum accenting, and the hi-hat or ride keeping time. The overall sound was different, not danceable, but instead was created for the listener. This was a new revolution in the world of jazz.

Below: Charlie Parker on sax, Thelonious Monk on keys.

Jump blues was an up-tempo blues played by a small group featuring the horn players and a heavy, insistent beat. These groups were often employed to take the place of the larger big bands to play in jitterbug rooms. Jump was made especially popular in the late 1940s and early 1950s, through artists such as Louis Jordan, Big Joe Turner, Roy Brown, Charles Brown, T-Bone Walker, Roy Milton, Billy Wright, and Wynonie Harris.

The next step was rock 'n' roll music. Songs like "Rock Around the Clock" were advertised as the "new" foxtrot music. However, so much of the early material that was played was actually jump blues and rockabilly.

CHAPTER TWENTY NINE: MUSICIANS' DRUGS

Musicians were not the only ones partaking of the easy access drugs of the era. However, their high profile lives made them role models for citizens who might have not chosen this path. The medical industry had not yet developed countercheck procedures in which to protect the public from overdose or addiction, and the general public and the government was simply not accustomed to regulating medical supplies, and seemed at a loss.

Marijuana was legal until 1937 in some states in the U.S. and jazz musicians that would partake were known as "vipers". These vipers traveled between New Orleans, Chicago, and Harlem, and felt that this Mexican drug was a great inspiration. Some of the famous vipers included Louis Armstrong and Buddy Bolden. Cab Callaway recorded the song "That Funny Reefer Man", while Fats Waller recorded the tune "The Viper Drag". In Storyville, New Orleans, pot was called moota. In the '30s marijuana cigarettes were called "muggles" or "reefers". Swing musicians that partook were called "cats," "alligators," or "ickeys."

Opium was legal in the early 1900s. Heroin, cocaine, and marijuana were sold right over the counter in every drug store, however opium dens were found in Chinatown. It is the users that are being talked about in the refrain of the popular 1909 tune "Chinatown, My Chinatown".

Strangers taking in the sights, pig-tails flying here and there
See that broken Wall Street sport, still thinks he's a millionaire,
Still thinks he's a millionaire,
Pipe-dreams banish every care.
Chinatown, my Chinatown, where the lights are low…

**Below: Two women and a man in a Chinatown opium den
in the late 19ᵗʰ century.**

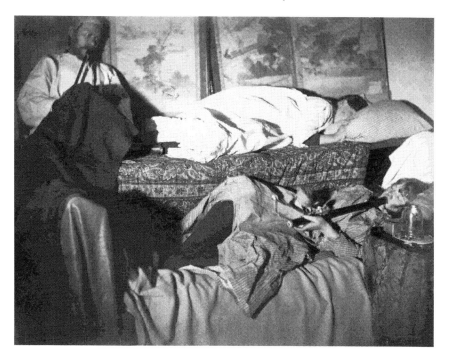

The patronage of opium dens was referred to as "kickin' the gong around" (as in the Cab Callaway hit song) because, when you wanted your pipe refilled, you summoned the attendant by hitting a gong. The clientele was often incapacitated to the point that they would be lucky if they could just manage to kick the gong at the foot of their bed or couch.

Below: Cab Calloway, "Kicking the gong around" in his "zoot suit".

CHAPTER THIRTY: CRAZY WASHBOARD BANDS

From the mid 1920s through to the '30s washboard bands received the nod from jazz audiences across the country. Here is a list of the ones that I know of. Washboard players, in place of a drummer, provided a good steady rhythm and have been traditionally seen in jazz, blues, zydeco, skiffle, spasm, jug band and in old-time music. It is of value just to see who was taking part in this craze as there were some very talented players in these washboard bands.

- **Jimmy Bertrand's Washboard Wizards** (1927)
  Jimmy Bertrand, washboard
  Louie Armstrong, cornet
  Johnny Dodds, clarinet
  Jimmy Blythe, piano

- **The Beale Street Washboard Band** (1929)
  Baby Dodds, washboard
  Johnny Dodds, clarinet
  Frank Melrose, piano
  Herb Moorland, trumpet

- **Blythe's Washboard Band** (1926)
  Jimmy Blythe, piano
  Johnny Dodds, clarinet
  W.E. Burton, washboard

- **Fowler's Washboard Wonders** (1925)
  Lemuel Fowler, piano
  Stanley Harding, washboard
  Percy Glascoe, clarinet and sax

- **Washboard Rhythm Kings** (1931) **(below)**

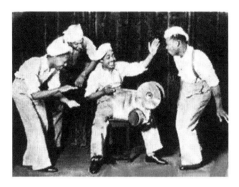

- **Blythe's Washboard Ragamuffins** (1926)
Jimmy Blythe, piano
Johnny Dodds, clarinet and sax
Trixie Smith, vocals
Jasper Taylor, washboard

Below: Johnny Dodds was respected by other musicians for his professionalism and virtuosity, and appreciated by audiences for his heartfelt, emotional style and delivery of the blues.

- **Wilton Crawley and the Washboard Rhythm Kings** (1930)
Bruce Johnson, washboard
Jelly Roll Morton, piano
Wilton Crawley, vocals and clarinet
Henry Allen, trumpet

- **Johnny Dodds Washboard Band** (1928) (**below**)
  Baby Dodds, washboard
  Johnny Dodds, clarinet
  Lil Hardin Armstrong, piano
  Bill Johnson, bass

- **The Hoosier Hot Shots** (1930 - 1970) (**below**)
  Hezzie Trietsch, washboard and slide whistle
  Gabe Ward, clarinet
  Ken Trietsch, tenor guitar
  Frank Kettering, upright bass

- **O'Bryants Famous Original Washboard Band** (1925)
  Jimmy O'Bryant, clarinet
  W. E. Burton, washboard and banjo
  Jimmy Blythe, piano

- **Scorpion Washboard Band** (1933)
  vocals, guitar, kazoo, washboard - artists unknown

- **Spike Jones and the City Slickers** (1940) (**below**)
  Spike Jones, washboard and sound effects
  with a 12 to 25 piece band

- **Original Washboard Band with Jasper Taylor** (1928)
  Johnny Dodds, clarinet
  Jasper Taylor, washboard
  Julian Davis, vocals
  Eddie Haywood, piano

- **Tug Jug Washboard Band** (1928)
  Thomas Dorsey, vocals
  Tampa Red, guitar and kazoo
  washboard – unknown artist

- **Clarence Williams Washboard Four** (1927)
  Clarence Williams, piano and vocals
  Floyd Casey, washboard

- **Clarence Williams Washboard Band** (1929)
  James P. Johnson, piano
  Clarence Williams, vocals
  Floyd Casey, washboard

Below: Clarence Williams is second from left at the piano.

- **Clarence Williams Washboard Five** (1928)
  King Oliver, cornet
  Clarence Williams, piano and vocals
  Floyd Casey, washboard

- **Dixie Jazzers Washboard Band/Dixie Washboard Band** (1927)
  Clarence Williams, piano and vocals
  Jasper Taylor, Floyd Casey, Bruce Johnson, washboard
  Ed Allen, cornet

Below: The washboard percussive set up created by the author and immortalized as "Kit of the Month" in Modern Drummer Magazine. This is played by Tony "Mad Fingers" McBride who is renowned as "The Canadian Washboard King".

The unique contraption is arranged around a 20 inch Rodgers bass drum and a vertically secured 14 inch snare, each being struck by a Ludwig Speed King Pedal. Filling out the rig is a 10 inch Gretch snare, Zildjian and Sabian splash cymbals, ice bells, temple blocks, tuned bulb horns, restaurant bells, cowbells, a train whistle, and a pair of custom-built back-to-back stainless steel washboards in a teak and oak frame. Playing the kit with a series of taps, sweeps, honks, and glancing blows, McBride wears leather gloves that have metal thimbles on the fingertips and copper plumbing end caps on the thumbs, enabling ten points of contact. Tony McBride supplies melody and countermelody, all within a strong percussive support.

CHAPTER THIRTY ONE:
THE STAGE MICROPHONE

The microphone was initially invented for use in the telephone, and perfected for that purpose on March 6, 1876. Without the creation of an amplifier and the addition of speakers to buildup the sound and transfer it to the listeners, the microphone would not work in a stage application. Consequently the industry had to wait until the 1930s.

In 1930, Rudy Vallee appears to have been the first major star to use a microphone to sing in a ballroom. Although it is uncertain how rapidly the sort of sound system he used became commonplace, others in the business surely noticed. In the 1934 recording of Bing Crosby singing "The Very Thought of You", the microphone picks up the slightest sound of his voice. If he sang that way unaided in a large hall, no one would have been able to hear him. The microphone enabled a gentler, more intimate delivery in public that before would have been suitable only in the privacy of someone's house. It allowed subtleties in the voice, creating a larger scope of emotion and intimacy. It let the performer sound breathy or sexual, and song delivery was greatly enhanced.

Below: In the 1930s Bing Crosby (left) and Rudy Vallee (right) introduce the microphone to the world of stage entertainment.

Powerhouse performers like Al Jolson and Bill Murray could walk out to the end of a stage with a thousand people in the audience and a seventeen piece orchestra playing, sing, and be heard. That was the type of powerful voice that was needed if you were to be a star. It took the microphone for us to appreciate Billy Holiday or Bing Crosby. When Crosby had his debut with the Paul Whitman Orchestra, Al Jolson was there to hear him. When Bing had finished Jolson leaned over to the press and said, "He had to use a microphone, must be a momma's boy." Little did the early stars know how much would change with the microphone.

Below: Frank Sinatra

I was the artistic director in 2004 in a vaudeville theatre that was built in 1927. When we took the building over we found a door to a room that was all concrete inside, forty feet long but only five feet wide. When I saw the huge 24 inch speaker mounted at the far end of the room, I went to the other end to find a vintage microphone mounted in that wall. This was the primitive echo chamber used for the stage. Sing into the microphone on stage and the sound would come out of the huge speaker in the long concrete room, travel to the end of the forty foot chamber, and be picked up by the microphone in the wall. The signal would then be added to the original mix coming out on stage and there was your echo effect. To this, the soundman could add as much effect as he wanted by just turning up the volume on that channel of the mixer. It was brilliant!

A variation of the microphone is the instrument pick-up. The type used on guitars were called transducers, and were first developed in 1924 with Gibson's contribution of the humbucking in 1932 (I have one and it is magnificent). Humbuckers employ two coils to "buck the hum" (or cancel out the interference) picked up by single coil pickups.

So while we have the public's ear changing from hot jazz to cool jazz in the form of swing music, because of these pickups, bands were now exchanging banjo players for guitar players. Previously, the guitar had been considered a parlour instrument and was much smaller than the guitars we use today, which lessened their output of volume. They could not be heard in a musical ensemble larger than four pieces. The "Spanish guitar" was yet to come into its own. Also out the door went the tubas to be replaced with the double bass or upright bass, or perhaps you want to call it the bass violin. These changes helped to customize the new sound.

Below: Gibson ES 150 – an example of an early 1930s electric guitar. The electric pick-up ("instrument microphone") is the horizontal bar laying beneath the strings, at the base of the fingerboard.

Some of the great banjo players of the day were pulling their hair out with this change. To the rescue came the Gibson Guitar Company who, in 1924, had created a new instrument called the tenor guitar. It was originally sold so banjo players could double on guitar, but now it was to save their career. The tenor guitar had a full size guitar body with, basically, a tenor banjo neck on it. Tuned like a tenor banjo which is in fifths, C D G A, the players were back on the job, and with a new mellow sound that fulfilled the guitar part, or complimented the regular six-string guitars.

CHAPTER THIRTY TWO:
RADIO PICTURES (SOME SAY TELEVISION)

Television was created by Scottish inventor John L. Baird in 1925. With only thirty lines of resolution you could barely make out a human face, but it was proof that his idea was working. He also invented the first video recording system. In 1927, a 21 year old inventor named Philo Taylor Farnsworth, from the United States, created electronic television: a system that could capture moving images in a form that could be coded onto radio waves, then transformed back into a picture on a screen. This was the direct ancestor of modern television.

The general public first envisioned the idea as "radio pictures". All through the 1930s there was a good deal of talk and speculation about this new medium that was being developed. In 1939, at the New York World's Fair, they displayed a working television set but, with the onslaught of WWII at their heels, production needed to wait until after the war. Television was to make an impact like nothing else had. With every wonderful thing there is always a downside and the suffering came in lost revenues in the movie industry and radio. Television sales rose from 6,000 in 1946 to some 12 million by 1951. By 1955 half of the homes in America had a television set.

**Below: early television sets. Top: RCA sold 1936-1937
Left: Predicta 1958-1959 Right: Muntz 1951**

Below: Admiral 1948

In 1947, we saw the beginning of full commercial television broadcasting. 1948 was the start of the Texaco Star Theatre, starring Milton Berle who became known as Uncle Miltie, the first major American television star. At the same time, children's programming brought us The Howdy Doody Show, and there were news programs. One news show was required, by contract with the sponsor tobacco company, to always have a burning cigarette visible within the camera shot. The Jack Benny Show jumped ship from radio to television in 1950. Amos and Andy also left radio and started in TV in 1951. The Red Skelton Show ran from 1951 to 1971. It was one of the top three longest running shows, second to Gunsmoke, and third to The Ed Sullivan Show which aired in 1948 and lasted until June of 1971.

The early years of television were not only shot in black and white, but also filmed live with no retakes, edits, or splices. What they did was what you got. Yes, that is what live means! And boy, did they have some embarrassing moments, but they also caught some spontaneous adrenalin driven magical moments. Just imagine the stress of going on camera for the first time, with the whole nation watching to see how you'll do.

Below: T.V. performer, Red Skelton

The live spontaneous laughter during the filming of the Red Skelton Show was so infectious and genuine that Red sold the laugh tracks to a man named Charles Douglas who, in turn, created the "Laff Box" in 1953. These recordings were used to beef up the audience reaction on other shows. Since Red Skelton often performed pantomimes, it was easy for Charlie to get nice, clean recordings of laughter and applause without any disruptive dialogue. The same system is used today, so when you are watching a show like Jerry Seinfeld, the audience you can hear is laughing at Red Skelton.

As you can see, with television being a new medium, they went with a formula already proven in order to ensure success, and that was vaudeville. The variety show was what we had on The Ed Sullivan Show, and when the first talk show aired in 1953, called The Tonight Show, host Steve Allen again presented variety. So did Uncle Miltie, Red Skelton, Sid Caesar, Abbot and Costello, Phil Silvers, and Jack Benny.

Below: Imogene Coca and Sid Caesar,
Left: Uncle Miltie (Milton Berle) Right: Phil Silvers

But new concepts were also presented, and ABC brought us Disneyland in 1954, and the following year was the premiere of The Mickey Mouse Club. From the two major networks, NBC and CBS, that were the dominant force during the 1950s, came the dramas: The Kraft Television Theater in 1947, Studio One in 1948, The U.S. Steel Hour in 1953, and Playhouse 90 in 1956.

I Love Lucy, the hugely successful situation comedy starring Lucille Ball and Desi Arnaz, was recorded for T.V. since its debut in 1951 until the final show in 1957. The Honeymooners, starring Jackie Gleason, was first broadcast in 1955 and only ran one season. In the mid '50s we found quiz shows like "You Bet Your Life" with Groucho Marx, and "What's My Line" with Fred Allen, to be very popular. The Three Stooges and Laurel and Hardy started getting their film shorts shown on television and the audience loved them.

The man hours spent in front of the television screen each day has increased as time has passed; eventually children will only know the outside from having seen it on television.

CHAPTER THIRTY THREE: ODDS AND ENDS
A SMATTERING OF BEMUSED THOUGHTS

Parlours: Parlour or parlor is a word that comes from the French "parler" and means "to speak". It denotes an audience chamber or speaking room. In the home, the parlour was the main room of the house.

At the turn of the century, we find that, during the 1910s (and earlier) people made do on their own. Examples would be that 95% of births took place at home, and when a family member died, the body was prepared for burial in the home. In those days, undertakers were simply carpenters and cabinet makers who built coffins and caskets to order. Coffins are body-shaped boxes (toe-pinchers) and caskets are rectangular-shaped boxes that open from head to waist presenting only a partial view of the body. They were used during the Civil War, as it was common for the soldiers to have lost a foot or leg.

Below: A casket (pictured) is different from a coffin. This is now the most commonly used container for viewing the deceased in North America.

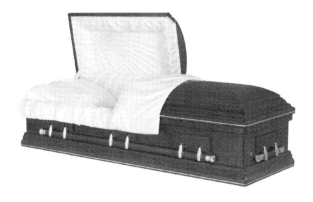

The body of the deceased was brought into the parlour, washed and clothed by the family, and it was common to have a group photograph taken with them and the rest of the family, or a portrait taken with them sitting up in a chair. Sometimes their eyes were left open; other times, once these death photos were developed, they would do a touch up on the photo to create the illusion that the eyes were opened and focused. There was also a contraption that could be rented that held the body in a standing position for the photograph. Prior to the Victorian era and the advent of photography, paintings of the dead were commissioned.

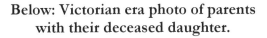

**Below: Victorian era photo of parents
with their deceased daughter.**

Because of this use, the parlour came to be also referred to as the "death room". At the end of WW1, influenza struck down millions of people, and so common were the dead bodies kept in the parlour, that the term "death room" had made its indelible mark on society.

Some ambitious undertakers, in an attempt to provide a more thorough service, advertised that they would remove this burden from the family home and provide all the needed preparations for the deceased, including final burial and service.

Below: Funeral parlour in Seattle (1900).

The magazine The Ladies Home Journal suggested that this wonderful service was the way of the future, and that these companies should be doing the thing previously done by the family in the parlour. With them supplying a "Funeral Parlour", the main family room in the home could now be considered the "living room", and be used not for mourning, but for socializing. Though the term "living room" was known as far back as 1825, it was not used commonly until this time, around 1918.

In no time at all, this system of arrangements for the dead caught on. The term parlour was forgotten in reference to the home and only remained in the common vocabulary to describe the funeral parlour, ice cream parlour, beauty parlour, billiards parlour, and pizza parlour.

Ukulele Ike: Cliff Edwards (Ukulele Ike), 1895 – 1971, was the voice of Jiminy Cricket and sang "When You Wish Upon a Star". His three octave range made him a popular vaudeville, radio, and film star. For years he was the ukulele player in a jug band called Fred Ozark's Jug Blowers. His original songs were "Fascinating Rhythm", "Toot, Toot, Toosie Goodbye", "Singing in the Rain", and "It's Only a Paper Moon". He sold 74 million records in his lifetime, made a number of films with Buster Keaton and Jack Benny, and in entirety appeared in over one hundred movies. He had his own national TV show, his own radio show, and a career with Walt Disney providing voiceovers and songs like "When I see an Elephant Fly" in Dumbo. Although once a millionaire, he died in 1971 in a California nursing home as an unknown. His body lay unclaimed for days.

Flagpole sitting: A fad that was born when stunt actor and former sailor Alvin "Shipwreck" Kelly, sat on a flagpole, either on a dare by a friend or as a publicity stunt. Shipwreck's initial 1924 sit lasted 13 hours and 13 minutes. It soon became a fad and other contestants set records of 12, 17 and 21 days. A small platform would be erected to accommodate a chair or cushion for the "sitter". In the year 1929, Shipwreck once again made the challenge for the title. He sat on a flagpole for 49 days in Atlantic City, New Jersey, setting a new record. The next year his record was broken when Bill Penfield, from Strawberry Point, Iowa, sat on a flagpole for 51 days and 20 hours, until a thunderstorm forced him to stop. Flagpole sitting in the 1920s was a major part of the decade. Most flagpole sitting died out after 1929, with the onset of the Great Depression.

Hokum: Originally called Oakum, Hokum refers to a type of American blues music. It consists of sexual innuendoes and is usually a comedic farce.

Royalty-free: In the U.S.A., any song written in 1922 or before is public domain. You can record it without paying royalties.

Coon songs: The most popular coon song of all time was entitled "All Coons Look alike to Me", written by Earnest Hogan, a Black man. Coon songs were popular to the point of being a national craze in the 1890s. They also became popular in Britain right through to the 1920s.

Stagger Lee: Stagalee or Stagolee was a popular song written in 1895 and tells the story of a murder on Christmas Eve in 1895. In a St. Louis saloon, "Stag" Lee Shelton, a Black pimp, shot William "Billy" Lyons. Eyewitnesses say Billy snatched Stag's Stetson hat. Boom, boom, boom, boom went Stag's .44. You don't mess with a man's hat. The song refers to William as "Billy the Lion" which was his nick name, but it often comes out sounding like Billy De Lyon. It's been recorded over four hundred times, with many variations of the story. The first recording was in 1923.

Passing: The song "On the Sunny Side of the Street" was written in 1929 and the subject matter was about "passing": Mulatto people passing as White people.

Roundelay: is a a short simple song with a refrain. An example would be "Coney Island Washboard Roundelay".

Miniature golf: Sometimes called garden golf, miniature gold was created in the early 1900s. In the early years it was played on real grass, and in the 1920s, bumpers or rails were added to confine the travel of the ball. A smoother playing surface was developed made of hard pressed cottonseed hulls, later to become artificial turf. Celebrities loved the game and that helped to spread its popularity. By 1930 there were more than 30,000 courses across the continent.

Monopoly: Charles B. Darrow created Monopoly in 1934 and when he offered the game to Parker Brothers they responded with a letter of rejection. He took it on his own to produce a small number of the games and they sold very fast. He then had five thousand games produced and sold them all to stores in Philadelphia. Parker Brothers changed their minds and, in 1935, started producing the game which sold twenty thousand sets in one week.

Betty Boop: In the early 1930s this was to be North America's first flapper icon. This cartoon's inspiration was the vocalist Helen Cane. With her spit curls and high baby voice she was known as the "Boop Oop a Doop" girl. Betty Boop would sometimes sing Helen's songs.

"The Story of Ella Speed": This was a popular song written in August, 1894

So, come on an' all take heed,
Let me tell you 'bout the death of poor Ella Speed

In regards to the song Ella Speed, we find that, in 1894, Ella was a twenty-eight year old Black or Mulatto prostitute living in a "sporting house" on what is now Iberville Street in the French Quarter. She was the object of the attentions of Louis Bill "Bull" Martin or Martini, a bartending Italian-American whom she had known for several months. He wanted to set her up in an apartment as his mistress, a common arrangement at the time. Ella, however, was not interested. She liked his money, but didn't care much for the man. Besides, she already had a husband, one Willie Speed.

Louis was a bully who had been arrested and tried on three separate occasions for assault and battery charges, and who, at the time of the murder, was wanted by the constable for another beating. Louis became enraged at the thought that she might be fond of another man (husband or not). One night, after a day spent drinking, she and Louis returned late to the bordello and, feeling quite drunk, retired at around 2:00 A.M. The next time Ella was seen was in the morning when she screamed and emerged from her room saying, "Help me, Louis shot me!" She collapsed in the hallway, just as the bordello's Madame spied Louis in the doorway, holding a smoking pistol. Louis disappeared, and soon an officer arrived, followed by an ambulance, but it was too late. Ella had been shot with the bullet piecing her heart, left lung, and liver, from which wounds she soon bled to death.

A manhunt begun in an attempt to find Louis who, after a day, turned himself in to the police captain. He was arrested, held, and charged with murder. After a trial, a jury found him guilty of manslaughter. He was sentenced to twenty years in prison.

The song "The Story of Ella Speed" appeared soon after the initial shooting and was based on newspaper accounts. The title is usually "Ella Speed" but it has also been "Bill Martin and Ella Speed".

It was recorded by Lead Belly several times between 1933 and 1950. It was also recorded by many others, and said to be the model for the song "Bully of the Town".

Folk: When we talk about folk music, folk songs, and folk dance, these are comparatively recent expressions. They are derived from the term folklore, which was instated in 1846. Folk music in North America means musical folklore with origins in the 19th century. It has been defined as: music transmitted by word of mouth, music of the lower classes, and music with no known composer. In the 1960s new songs were written, recorded, and performed that took on the definition and were described as folk music, and that became a temporary popular trend.

CHAPTER THIRTY FOUR:
BLUES AND JAZZ INSTRUMENTS

Drums: The drum set was invented by jazz and jug band musicians. Before the establishment of "the drum set" the snare was played by one person and the bass drum was played by another. There were also side drums which were the equivalent to a tom tom drum or floor tom. The most common bands during the later part of the 19th century were marching bands. As bands began to play for more indoor public events, it was cost efficient to have only one drummer. At first a bass drum was mounted on the back of the snare player and operated by beaters pulled by strings on the players elbows (one-man band style). This was known as the "contraption", a name later shortened to "traps". Playing indoors also saw New Orleans musicians begin experimenting by using fly swatters in place of sticks, which later became wire brushes.

Since everyone kept the beat with their foot it caused a few of the new novelty bands to try playing the bass drum by kicking it. Baby Dodds (famous jug band washboard player, and the man credited as the father of traditional jazz drumming) was the innovator of this concept and would arrive early enough that the stage manager wouldn't see him pound two nails in the stage to stop his bass drum from sliding forward. Then he would kick it with the toe of his shoe (inventing and coining the term kick-drum) while playing the snare which sat on a small table and a cymbal with his sticks. (he also played the table) One of the players, aware of this method, was a lad named William F. Ludwig who had started making his own drums. He invented the bass drum pedal and applied for a patent in 1909.

The next invention that was to change drumming didn't come until the 1920s when we were to see Baby Dodds using a "low-boy". This was a pedal he created that closed two cymbals and stood twelve inches high. Prior to this, he used to tie a cymbal to the bottom of his foot, and tap another cymbal he had nailed to the floor. Before the low-boy, drummers would accent the weak beats on two and four by choking or muting a suspended cymbal with their hand. Now this accent could be played with the foot, freeing up a players hands to perform syncopated rhythms. This advancement helped create the four-way independence texture that drummers use today.

Baby Dodds also created rim shots, and he played the sides of his drums, and often played the surfaces of the entire stage during solos. At this time no other drummer did solos. He had a shallow floor tom that sat on the floor to his left, and he would put his left foot on it pressing down to change the pitch while playing a roll on it with his sticks. He also invented the ride cymbal pattern that is commonly used today.

Below: Drummer Stan Farmer.
Notice the low boy under his right foot.

Having once been burglarized, Dodds arrived at a prestigious concert with no drum kit. He walked in carrying a kitchen chair, proceeded to break the two back spindles out of the chair to use as drum sticks, and played the chair. Some people were overheard to have said that they preferred the chair to the sound of the drums.

Born in New Orleans on Christmas eve, Warren "Baby Dodds" had an older brother, Johnny Dodds, the famous clarinetist. Baby played with the King Oliver's Creole Jazz Band, Jelly Roll Morton's Red Hot Peppers, and Louis Armstrong's Hot Seven. He started out playing in Frankie Dusen's Eagle Band on washboard in 1914, and was to become the first great drummer of jazz. Baby Dodds taught George Wettling and Gene Krupa all of their stick technique, and was the inspiration behind Max Roach becoming a drummer. Rhythm Magazine calls him "The number one most influential drummer of all time."

The "low-boy" was elevated twice during its development from 12" to the 20" tall "sock-cymbal" to the standard "high hat" as drummers like Gene Krupa wanted the option of playing time on the cymbals with their hands.

In 1934, Gene Krupa, playing with the Benny Goodman orchestra, developed and set the standards for what would become the traditional drum kit today (with the exception of the bass drum size): 24-26" bass drum, 14" snare, 9x13 small tom mounted on the shell of the bass drum, and a 16" floor tom. He was also responsible for the white marine pearl finish on his kit which everyone copied, including Buddy Rich. Prior to that, all drums had been either plain white or black. Gene played the first extended drum solos to high critical acclaim but, master though he was, he could not (so it's said) hold a stick to Buddy Rich.

I experienced the thrill of performing with Buddy Rich, and his story is worth briefly telling. Buddy was a vaudeville star at the age of 18 months old and billed as "Traps, the Drum Wonder". At the time he was the second highest paid child star in the world (after Jackie Coogan). By the age of eleven he was performing as a bandleader. Buddy had no formal training and never practiced; he only played during performances. He hired a stand-in so his band could rehearse. He was a great guy, straight forward, honest and generous.

The Trumpet and Cornet: The trumpet is one of the oldest instruments dating back to 1500 B.C. It is commonly a Bb instrument and the highest register in the brass family. In 1814, the valves were added to the trumpet to enable it to play the chromatic scale evenly.

Being the loudest solo instrument, it was the lead instrument in early jazz.

**Below: Louis Armstrong's trumpet,
given to him by King George V in 1933.**

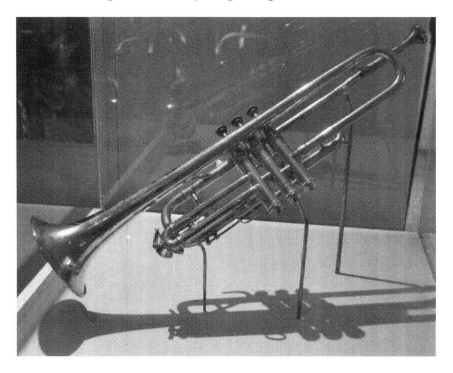

The Cornet has a warmer, more mellow tone than the trumpet, although the technique involved in playing both instruments is very much the same. Both instruments are pitched in Bb. The cornet is available in a model called the Shepherd's Crook, which is a shorter horn that provides better balance when holding the instrument. This is the most popular choice for traditional players. There is also a long model cornet with a brighter sound that looks closer to the trumpet, and is commonly used in concert bands. Also available is an Eb Soprano model pitched a fourth above the standard Bb model and used mostly in brass bands.

Some of the great jazz players were Buddy Bolden, Frankie Keppard, Louis Armstrong, Red Nichols, Bix Beiderbecke and Miles Davis (All of whom played the cornet, and some, the trumpet.)

Saxophone: The Sax is in the family of woodwind instruments. Saxophones are usually made of brass and played with a single-reed mouthpiece similar to that of the clarinet. It was invented by Adolphe Sax in 1840 in Belgian. He patented the saxophone in 1846. Coleman Hawkins was the first American jazz saxophonist to become famous during the

1920s-'30s. Jimmy Dorsey and Johnny Hodges also had major success.

Below: a 1930s silver-plated "Pennsylvania Special" alto saxophone created by Kohlert & Sons for Selmer.

Trombone: This is an instrument in the brass family usually pitched in Bb. It appeared in Europe in the 15th century. The first use in a symphony was in 1807. Edward "Kid" Ory had the genius idea to apply the magic of trombone to jazz. He played with a huge list of who's-who in the jazz community. Miff Mole is another player who was extremely successful on the trombone.

Clarinet: The clarinet is in the woodwind family and is commonly a Bb instrument. Clarinet bodies have been made from a variety of materials including wood, plastic, hard rubber, metal, resin, and ivory. The role of the clarinet is to embellish the melody. Here is a list of prominent players from the '20s and '30s: Benny Goodman, Pete Fountain, Artie Shaw, Johnny Dodds, Bill Johnson, Ted Lewis, Don Redman, Omer Simeon, Gene Woods, Barney Bigard, Jimmy Dorsey, Jimmie Noone, and Pee Wee Russell.

Below: Tommy and Jimmy Dorsey. The two brothers fought constantly, and eventually separated to create their own bands.

Below: Benny Goodman on clarinet.

Banjo: There are several theories whereupon historians attempt to connect the North American banjo to a variety of African musical instruments. The results are always the same and leaves them pointing to an example of stringed instrument that is not a banjo, but incorporates some similarities. I am quicker to believe the name banjo was inspired by the name of an African instrument, than to credit the creation of the instrument itself to anyone other than the people who built them in the United States. Whether these people were Black or White, the banjo is an American instrument.

In 1777, we have the first mention of a five-string instrument with the added peg half way up the neck. These instruments were fretless and very difficult to keep in tune. In Jamaica, there were African instruments referred to as a strum-strum, banza, banjer or banjars. They were also, at some time, referred to as an akontin. However, these were no more similar to the American banjo than the lute or mandolin. In 1621 they were using the term banza: in 1754 banjar: in 1776 we find a similar instrument being referred to as the banjo, although it was not a banjo. Again in 1781 notations and letters were found calling it the banjar. I have heard historians claim that in 1654, the banjo is mentioned in Jamaica, and that in 1774 the term merrywang is used to describe the instrument.

In addition to the "banjar" theory, there is another theory: Historians link the banjos origins to the Griots (West African storytellers) located in the Senegambia region of West Africa. The Griots used an instrument called a xalam (pronounced halam), and some historians now believe it is the ancestor of the banjo. Enslaved Africans from the Wolof community brought the knowledge of the xalam to the new world. They were the largest ethnic group in Senegal, and the first to be enslaved. The xalam is a member of the lute family and was a five-string instrument. The body of the instrument was more oblong than round like the banjo. The head was made out of calf or iguana skin, both being very thin, and the strings were made out of calf skin.

In conclusion, these instruments were called by a lot of different names, depending upon where you lived. They were describing a number of African instruments that were in various states of evolution. None of these instruments were the American banjo. Were they an inspiration? Most likely, but they were not the end product. This equates to holding up a blow gun which fires a projectile and must be pointed at the target and trying to lay claim on inventing the Winchester rifle.

From the 1740s to the mid 19th century, African- Americans were seen as the primary players of the banjo. Until the early 1800s, the banjo was seen as an instrument for the lower classes. In the mid-1800s, the banjo gained popularity. In the mid-1800s the S.S. Stewart Company began mass producing banjos that were popular and affordable for the mid-economic classes.

- In 1843, the first documented minstrel show by Dan Emmett & Virginia Minstrels showcased two banjos.

- In 1857, metal strings were invented. It seems they were cheaper than the normal professionally made gut-strings, and lasted longer than the homemade fiber or gut variety.

- In 1860s-1870s, the first closed-back banjos, and first top tension banjos were marketed by Dobson (i.e. Buckbee) in the U.S. & England

- In 1863-1897, James H. Buckbee Co. of New York was the largest banjo maker.

- In 1878-1904, the S.S. Stewart Co. of Philadelphia made 25,000 banjos!

- In 1881, Dobson patented a tone ring. The ring creates sustain.

- In 1894, the first patent was applied for a banjo mute.

- In 1894, the first Grover bridge patent was received.

- In 1907, J.B. Schall of Chicago invented the tenor banjo - or four-string banjo - tuned like a mandolin. Later this tuning was to drop a note from mandolin tuning of GDAE to CGDA. This made it tuned like a cello, which remains the standard tuning today.

- In 1909, the Vega Instrument Company created the Tubaphone banjo.

- In 1910, the tango dance and music craze reached America; the tenor banjo was sold as the "tango banjo".

- In 1919, the four-string bass banjo - or cello banjo - was created. Gibson began manufacturing a four-string cello banjo, known as the CB-4. Some of the other vintage manufacturers of four-string bass banjos include Bacon & Day. Gold Tone is the only contemporary manufacturer.

**Below: the Gibson Bass Banjo
"the Noblest Instrument of Them All"**

The Gibson Bass Banjo

—"The Noblest Instrument of Them All"

Because of its unusual size and striking appearance the new Gibson Bass Banjo compels instant attention, wherever used — and when the majestic tones of its deep, powerful voice boom out none can resist its magic spell.

Never before has a bass banjo of this type been considered as a practical possiblity — yet the skill and wisdom of Gibson Craftsmen have found the way to build such an instrument, one that is not only practical but practically indispensable in banjo bands, either small or large.

Few instruments can yield greater pleasure to either player or audience than this great bass. For real rhythm it has no substitute. Its foundation tones form a rich carpet upon which to spread the melodic voices of the higher pitched instruments.

Beautifully finished in ivory with solid pearloid peg head inlaid with vari-colored rhinestones. Specially selected white calfskin head. All metal parts finished in glistening gun metal.

The New Gibson Bass Banjo is tuned and played the same as the mando-bass - G-D-A-E.

The young lady playing the bass banjo illustrated here is a member of Miss Jean Rankins' famous all-girl orchestra known as "The Blue Belles." The orchestra is considered one of the top-notchers in vaudeville.

Famous orchestra leaders welcome the new Gibson Bass Banjo

- In 1918, the first Gibson banjos were produced, and in 1921 the first modern flange and resonator banjos were made by William Lange & Paramount Banjos.

- In 1921, McHugh of the Gibson Company patented adjustable truss rods for guitars and mandolins, also, adjustable tension rods and adjustable bridges for banjos. In 1923 we saw the first geared tuners patented by C. Kremp.

- In 1925, Gibson Mastertone banjo was introduced to the marketplace.

**Below: the author displaying his
1931 Gibson Mastertone tenor banjo.**

- In 1929, modern banjo armrests were invented by L.A. Elkington.

- In 1930-1945, the five-string banjo almost disappears as there were no strings available.

- In the 1950s, plastic heads become available and they are unaffected by temperature. Prior to this development, banjos had calf-skin heads and, when the banjo had been exposed to high humidity, the head had to be tightened and, if it had just been brought in from outside, as the instrument warmed up the head would need to be loosened or it would split. This produced constant tuning problems that were eliminated with the synthetic head.
- Some of the great players would include: Harry Reser, Eddie Lang, Eddie Peabody, Johnny St. Cyr, Nick Lucas, Eddie Condon, Maurice Bolyer, Uncle Dave Macon, Ikey Robinson, Fred Guy, Bill Eastwood, Bob Gillette, Arthur Taylor, and Charles Bocage.
- Henry Heanon Slingerland created the Slingerland Manufacturing Company which gained momentum in 1914 and was established by 1923 building ukuleles, banjos, and guitars. At some time between 1924 and 1928, they changed the name to the Slingerland Banjo Company. The popularity of the banjo caused the Ludwig Drum Company to begin building banjos, which infuriated Henry Slingerland and so he began building and selling drums in an effort to financially crush the Ludwigs: which he did. Slingerland changed their name to the Slingerland Banjo and Drum Company in 1928, and were to become the largest manufacturer of drums in the world.
- In the 1960s, when the folk boom hit, Gibson and Vega were the only companies to still have banjos in their catalogues as compared to two hundred banjo manufacturers in the early 1900s.
- Today, the tenor banjo has all but disappeared from music stores in North America where they have not been sold for the last twenty years. It is unusual to even find a music store salesperson who knows what a tenor banjo is.

Types of banjos:
- The standard five-string banjo is a twenty two-fret instrument, with a scale length of 26 ¼". It is usually tuned to open G (G,D,G,B,D) tuning.
- The long neck five-string has a scale length of 32 and 7/64ths of an

inch, with twenty five frets. It is usually tuned to open E (E,B,E.G#,B). This was the banjo played and created by Pete Seeger in 1943.

- The plectrum banjo is a four-string that commonly has twenty two frets and is tuned in C (C,G,B,D)
- The tenor banjo is a four-string with 17 to 19 frets and is tuned in fifths (C,G,D,A). Designed for traditional Dixieland jazz, it is often tuned up a note (G,D,A,E - like a mandolin but an octave lower) and used for Irish music.
- Other examples are considered by many to by bastardized hybrids. They include the guitar-banjo, banjo-ukulele, banjo-mandolin, and the twelve-string guitar-banjo

Violin: This is a four-string instrument, tuned in fifths as GDAE. It is also referred to as the fiddle. In North American music we find that the violin was the original lead instrument in the earliest blues bands. The hillbilly, hokum, and country bands also featured the violin as main instruments. It is played with a bow or by plucking the strings with the right hand, and is the highest pitched instrument in the viol family which takes in the viola, cello, and double bass.

Joe Venuti, one of the first great jazz violinists, is known as the father of jazz violin. He is admired for his work during the 1920s with guitarist Eddie Lang, who played six-string and tenor guitar. Joe Venuti also was in the Paul Whiteman Orchestra, and was best friends with Bix Beiderbecke the cornetist.

The violin's sound is closer to the sound of the human voice than any other instrument, and it blends and accents vocals, creating a soothing or dynamic effect when applied in that manner.

Vibraphone: The vibraphone was created in 1921 and used steel bars. In 1928 the vibraharp was created with aluminum bars, giving it a more mellow sound and considerably reducing the weight of the instrucment, as well as several other improvements over the first model. These instruments were used in playing the popular jazz music of the day. The instrument was made by the Leedy Manufacturing Company and it achieved a degree of popularity after it was used in the novelty recordings of "Aloha 'Oe" and "Gypsy Love Song" by vaudeville performer Louis Frank Chiha (stage name: Signor Frisco).

**Below: The vibraphone, or "Vibes",
is played with four mallets.**

The Guitar: The guitar is typically a six-string instrument, however, there are also twelve-string guitars, harp guitars, and tenor guitars with four strings. The acoustic guitar can be broken down into several categories: classical guitars (nylon, silk, or gut strings) also known as Spanish guitars; flamenco guitars (also nylon strings); Hawaiian guitars or lap steels guitars (1885); and arch-top and flat-top acoustic guitars. There is also a resonator, or Dobro guitar that was designed to produce more volume.

The guitar was considered a parlour instrument, as the volume was too low to allow it to be heard in a band situation until 1928 when the electric guitar pick-up was created.

**Below: is a Gibson six-string and
the author's Gibson four-string tenor guitar.**

Early influential guitarists in blues and jazz were: Eddie Lang, Robert Johnson, Charlie Christian, T-Bone Walker, Les Paul, Lonnie Johnson, Blind Lemon Jefferson, Blind Arthur Blake, Lead Belly, Big Bill Broonzy, Freddie Green, George Van Eps, and Carl Kress.

In 1935, the musical trend had fully moved towards swing music, which was simply a style of Jazz, but this new sound had no room for the banjo which had been a main component in hot jazz. High profile banjo players would have been left out in the cold had it not been for the creation of the tenor guitar: a full size guitar with a banjo neck, tuned like a cello or tenor banjo.

In 1924, the Gibson Company created the tenor guitar with an oval body shape. It was first manufactured to allow the banjo player to double on guitar. Gibson replaced the oval body shape with a true guitar shape in 1927. At this same time the Martin Guitar Company also began producing tenor guitars. In the 1920s the tenor banjo was the most popular instrument, there were thousands of tenor players, so the idea of producing a guitar that all of them could play opened a huge market of potential buyers, and was a windfall for Gibson. Players in the musician's union were increasing their paycheques playing these new tenor guitars which fell under the category of "doubling" (playing a second instrument).

When hot jazz was to evolve into swing, the tenor banjo player was out the door. But with the tenor guitar, once again the banjo players were employed and providing a very unique sound that also worked well in accompaniment to a six-string guitar. The tenor guitar was to see a short lifespan during this era, but not extinction. It came into limited play again during the 1960s folk era. Today, the tenor guitar is again receiving the appreciation it deserves thanks to performing artist Mark Josephs. He created and runs the annual Tenor Guitar Gathering in Astoria, Oregon. Players and fans from all over the world come every year to this charming seaside town to experience four days of incredible concerts and workshops.

In 1924, Gibson created the first guitar pickup, passing sound through the bridge to be picked up by a magnet and coil. But it was not until 1932, when Adolph Rickenbacker created what he called "the frying pan" - a Hawaiian guitar with electromagnetic pickups - that the true electric guitar became possible.

The hummbucker coil was produced in 1934 by Electro Voice, but Seth Lover of Gibson was also working on the production of the hummbucker double-coil pickup and claimed to have it in 1932. As to who really created it first is still argued, however Seth Lover of Gibson did apply for the patent and received it, crediting him for the creation and rights to build and sell the hummbucker. It was the driving force behind the sales of the 1955 Les Paul electric guitar.

Kazoo: Invented in 1840, a patent was applied for in 1883 changing the name "membranophone" to "kazoo". In 1902, the submarine shaped kazoo was commercialized. The kazoo is an instrument which modifies its player's voice by way of a vibrating membrane. This was a common lead instrument in blues, jug and spasm bands in the late 19th and early 20th century. The Mound City Blue Blowers were the first to record with a kazoo and had several kazoo hits. The Original Dixieland Jass band recorded the song "Crazy Blues" with a kazoo solo. The Paul Whitman Orchestra used kazoo solos, and The Mills Brothers started out as a kazoo quartet in vaudeville. The Jelly Roll Morton Jazz Trio consisted of piano, kazoo and clarinet.

Tuba and Sousaphone: The tuba is the largest and lowest pitched brass instrument. It is often known as the brass bass (like the double bass is known as the string bass). There are different sizes of tubas. The tuba has been in jazz from the very beginning, and is only occasionally replaced by the sousaphone.

The sousaphone was developed in the 1890s by John Philip Sousa to do the job of the tuba, but it was shaped to wrap around the body with the weight supported by the left shoulder. It had a larger throat that would produce a warmer sound. Not originally designed for marching bands, it soon became the favorite choice as it projected the sound forward over the heads of the musicians in front, and was less fatiguing to carry.

**Below: On sousaphone is the great Sherwood Noble
(the author is on the left – both men were members of the
Banjo Palace house band, Gastown, B.C.)**

Below: Bob Stewart on tuba

Theatre Organ: The Mighty Wurlitzer pipe organ was created for silent movie theatres. The design was an attempt to install a one-man orchestra to handle the movie score. The company was founded in 1853.

Pump organ: The pump organ, or harmonium, is a type of reed organ that generates sound with foot-pumped bellows. These were very popular in the 1920s and '30s . Thomas "Fats" Waller began his career with a pump organ and recorded several times with one.

Piano: The word piano is a shortened form of pianoforte, and was created in 1655. The piano was there right at the beginning of the European colonization of America, and was a consistent element within the average home to unite a family musically and socially. The 1880s saw it as a ladies instrument, but that was to change as ragtime was developed, and the piano helped to take us into the jazz era. This wonderful instrument allowed the performer to play melody and chords simultaneously, and be able to deliver a bass line as well. Some early pianos were equipped with drums built right into them. The upright piano was created in 1805, because it had a smaller footprint and was somewhat portable. It became the most common.

Some of the great early influential pianists were: James P. Johnson, Scott Joplin, Fats Waller, Earl Hines, Eubie Blake, Fletcher Henderson, Jelly Roll Morton, Jimmy Blythe, Tom Turpin, Arthur Marshal, Scott Hayden, Artie Matthews, Art Tatum, and Teddy Wilson.

The Calliope: The calliope (steam piano), played with canvas gloves, would be heard aboard the first show boat, the "floating theatre", of 1831. Docking on the shores of different towns along the Mississippi, it provided a family performance of song, dance, minstrelsy, circus acts, and sometimes the demonstration of a doctor's "miracle tonic". The entertainment was brought to areas that had never had such a thing before, and was considered a delight.

The music was made by steam going through large whistles. Originally they used locomotive whistles that were all tuned to the desired pitch. The calliope was very loud! The notes are triggered by playing a 32 note piano-like keyboard. If you are in New Orleans, go to the French Quarter and at 11:00 A.M., you will hear the sound of the calliope on the Natchez River Boat, which is one of four ships on the Mississippi that still have an old calliope. Run down to the Toulouse Street Wharf and get aboard.

Below: the calliope whistles on the Steamboat Natchez

Double Bass: The double bass, or upright bass, also called the string bass, bass fiddle, bass violin, doghouse bass, contrabass, bass viol, stand-up bass, bull fiddle, or bass, is the largest and lowest-pitched bowed string instrument of the viol family. It is tuned EADG, hence, it is tuned in fourths, the only modern bowed instrument that is tuned this way. It is played with a bow or by plucking the strings, and originated in the 15th century.

Below: John Pattitucci on bass

CHAPTER THIRTY FIVE: FISTICUFFS

Bare knuckle prize fights, pugilism, fisticuffs, or boxing became popular in North America in the 1850s, and at that time there were no rules, no weight divisions, no referees, and no round limits. What was considered a sport to the participants was entertainment to the audience; sideshow entertainment at its best. Illegal in most communities, it was conducted quite often at remote locations in attempt to avoid local complaints that would cause the police to interrupt the exhibition.

British fighters began touring North America, challenging any and all street fighters to step into the "ring" which was a circle scraped in the dirt that the fighters were to stay within. Or sometimes the boundary was designated by a rope laid on the ground in a circle. The challenge was given: anyone accepting would throw in their hat (hence, tossing one's hat in the ring). The Irish-American could not resist the challenge, and had a natural talent since they had a pub tradition called "the Irish Stand Down" or "strap fighting". The stand down involved tying the two participants into chairs facing each other. They would trade punches until one was unconscious or dead, the other was considered the winner. The Irish loved to fight.

Eventually, some fisticuff rules were developed, as the fights had been so brutal that it was necessary in order to keep the public's interest. The early rules included: the fighters were stripped to the waist and did not wear gloves; kicking, biting and gouging of eyes was not permitted; punching or grabbing below the waist was also not allowed. Wrestling however was an essential part, and the opponent could be knocked or thrown to the ground, either by picking him up around the waist, or by a popular move known as cross buttock (knocking him down by running into him). Having thrown an opponent to the floor, the fighter was allowed to fall on top of him as heavily as possible. You were not allowed to punch or kick him once he was down, you could only fall on him. Once a man was down, there was a thirty second break before the next round, at which time someone would whistle or hit a gong. There was no limitation as to the number of rounds, and no referee; it was up to the audience to keep things right. The crowd gambled on the outcome of the match, and a good deal of money changed hands.

Later, when it was realized that a circle scraped in the dirt was not defined enough, four posts were put in with a rope running around the outside of the posts. Although it was now a square, it is still referred to as a ring today. The two fighters occupied diagonal corners, and each had two assistants. One used his knees as a seat for the boxer to sit on between rounds, and the other was the bottle man who gave the fighter a drink to help revive him.

The term "stake money" refers to a bag containing the bets, which was tied to the corner stake, so the audience could see that no one had run off with the cash. A line was scratched across the centre of the ring and this is where the boxers met to start the match: it was referred to as "toeing the line". They would start each new round that way. If one of the participants couldn't make it to the centre without help, it was said he "wasn't up to scratch".

In the United States, the first American champion was John Lawrence Sullivan, and he gained the title of "The Heavyweight Champion of the World." In the late 1800s, the police in some districts began to allow fights. The rules then changed to "Queensbury Rules," and fighters began to wear gloves. In 1892, Sullivan was defeated by Jim Corbett. Jim was from a new generation of boxers and had not cut his teeth fighting in the streets like his predecessors: he had been trained by a coach. Jim had a bit of an education, and dressed very well, gaining him the moniker of "Gentleman Jim Corbett." Jim's new technique of stepping and constantly moving, which he referred to as his scientific boxing technique, allowed him to avoid John L. Sullivan, and wear him down with jabs, eventually knocking him out in the twenty-first round, making Gentleman Jim the Heavyweight Champion of the World.

The new Queensbury rules were as follows:

1. Fighters are to wear mufflers or boxing gloves, and no shoes or boots with spikes will be allowed.

2. No wrestling or hugging is allowed.

3. The rounds are to be three minutes long with one minute of rest between rounds.

4. If either man falls through weakness or otherwise, he must get up unassisted, ten seconds to be allowed him to do so. The other man meanwhile to return to his corner, and when the fallen man is on his legs, the round is to be resumed and continued until the three minutes have expired. If one man fails to come to the scratch in the 10 seconds allowed, it shall be in the power of the referee to give his award in favor of the other man.

5. A man on one knee is considered down and, if struck, is entitled to the stakes.

6. Should a glove burst, or come off, it must be replaced to the referee's satisfaction.

7. You could not strike an opponent once they went down, nor could you hit below the belt, gouge their eyes, butt their head, or throttle their neck. A round ended when one of the boxers was knocked down or ruled "out" by a referee.

The Queensbury Rules put an end to the prizefighting heyday and transitioned the United States into the golden era of boxing. By 1920, legislation was passed that allowed public boxing matches; fighters, such as Jack Dempsey and Joe Louis, became sports icons.

**Below: John L. Sullivan, Gentleman Jim Corbett, Bob Fitzsimmons
Sullivan was beaten by Corbett, who was beaten by Fitzsimmons**

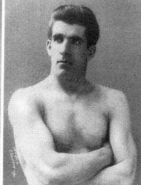

CHAPTER THIRTY SIX: STEAMBOATS

A paddlewheeler refers to two styles of ships propelled by a steam engine turning paddle wheels: one driven by a single wheel at the rear of the ship called a stern-wheeler, the other by two paddle wheels – one on each side - known as a side-wheeler. These flat bottomed ships were designed to navigate rivers; they were a major form of transportation up and down the Mississippi and Ohio Rivers. Later, the wheel was found to be less efficient than the screw propeller, but it far surpassed rowing and wind power by sail in its consistency of speed and reliance.

Below: the paddle wheel of the New Orleans based Natchez.

The paddlewheel steamboat first appeared in North America for use on the Delaware River in 1787. Hundreds of boats worked the Mississippi River system between 1830 and 1870.

The first paddlewheeler on the Ohio River was in 1812, and it opened up that region to traffic that helped develop the economic structure, creating a centre of river commerce and trade. More than 8,000 steamboats docked at Cincinnati in 1852. The ones that were not transporting freight were providing passengers a most wondrous and memorable experience.

The era of the steamboat introduced the idea of unprecedented speed into the American consciousness. Suddenly, transportation was not dependant on river current, instead, all rested on the power of the boiling steam engine, and the bravado of those captains who had the nerve to take the pressure of the boilers to their utmost limits, closing off the safety valves to ensure the fastest travel time. Not surprisingly, steamboat captains became known as daredevils, and they raced each other for titles. Who would own the route from New Orleans to St. Louis, from Natchez to Louisville? Best time in 1817 was 25 days, but by 1828 it was 8 days, 17 hours. The engines were continuously improved, and by 1843 the boat "Saltana" cut the time down to 4 days, 22 hours.

In the fifteen years before the Civil War, over five hundred passenger boats thrashed through river waters, faster and faster. People began to think that the main reason the steamboats existed was to race. Safety valves were weighted down with lead - or tied off with cables- to ensure that they would not impede the pressure. Even the betting public often helped feed the furnaces by shoveling in wood, resin, pitch, or anything that would increase the intensity of the fire for more speed. It is no wonder that so many steamboats were to blow up during races, resulting in an enormous loss of life.

Racing on the river was in full swing, and fortunes were wagered on who was the fastest. Outrageous amounts of money, property, cattle, and businesses were won and lost by the outcome of river races.

The world's most famous steamboat race of all was the one between the Natchez and the Robert E. Lee, from New Orleans to St. Louis.

The Battle of the Natchez and the Robert E. Lee

Captain Thomas P. Leathers had the Natchez, and he was a very colourful character. He was a considerable showman, but he was reckless and known for his grandstand plays when racing. His outrageous displays worked in his favour by filling his ship with people who preferred to be aboard with such a infamous captain. This man wrote the book on dirty tricks. He threw slabs of bacon fat and tubs of hog fat into his boilers for that final burst of speed; cut across his rivals' bows to make them slow down; and occasionally shot a cannon ball across the forward part of a steamer to vex her captain and amuse his own passengers and the audiences on shore.

In time, Leathers owned a succession of boats, each called Natchez, each one showier and speedier than its predecessor. He was so sure of himself he would occasionally let a rival steamer leave before the Natchez, then overtake it, and glide by while multitudes along the banks roared their admiration. In 1855, the speed of his fourth Natchez, in his eyes, made him lord of the river.

Launched in 1866, the Robert E. Lee, captained by a man named Cannon, soon won acclaim for her speed. Captain Leathers boasted of his sixth Natchez, launched in 1869, that she was the fastest thing on the river, and he, the greatest captain. The day came when Leathers and Cannon challenged each other to race. The newspapers were divided as to who might win, as the Robert E. Lee was undoubtedly a very good contender for the title. The captains set the date of the race for June 30, 1870.

North America, and most of Europe, took in every word the press could write concerning the race. Saloons, bars, and pubs saw punches exchanged arguing over the merits of each contender. Fortunes were wagered in all major cities. London, Paris, Boston, New York, and Philadelphia sent newspaper reporters to New Orleans and St. Louis to cover the race, and transmit their gossip and facts back home by wire.

A few days prior to the race, Captain Cannon had his crew strip the Robert E. Lee down to its bare hull. Every spare piece of wood and metal, all draperies, chandeliers, furniture, and fixtures were removed, and all cargo refused.

Captain Leathers, however, the boastful showman that he was, not only carried the Natchez's scheduled passengers and freight, but also made the flamboyant gesture of accepting the passengers and freight the Robert E. Lee had refused. He also provided special seats for the press. Both captains took the precaution of loading up on large barrels and boxes of lard, bacon fat, pine, resin, candle wax, pitch, and, as was usual in these contests, arranged for coal barges to stand by along the course.

The starting gun shot was fired at exactly 5 P.M.

The Robert E. Lee lurched ahead, while the Natchez lay calm, its captain leisurely finishing his cigar. Four minutes later, Captain Leathers gave orders for the Natchez to enter the race. Thousands of spectators, red in the face and screaming themselves hoarse, cheered as the Natchez pulled out.

Men with pocket watches were lined up in advantageous locations, each timing the ships' progress and dashing to telegraphs to relay their findings.

When the Natchez passed Baton Rouge at 8:31 P.M., the Robert E. Lee was six minutes ahead of her.

Captain Leathers held to his regular schedule, delivering passengers - who scooted ashore in all haste - and freight - which the roustabouts unloaded from the Natchez in record time. The Robert E. Lee made no stops.

The Natchez was still making good time and gaining on the adversary when Captain Cannon did the unexpected. Waiting to rendezvous with the Robert E. Lee was the steamboat, the Frank Pargaud. She rested about midstream of the course, and was loaded to the gunwales with tubs of lard, pine, and other combustibles. The Lee signaled. The Pargaud pulled parallel with the Lee. The Lee slowed down briefly while all hands rushed to lash the two ships together. The Pargaud kept its engines running to slow the Lee as little as possible while supplies were shifted, from the Pargaud to the Lee, at breakneck speed. Then, the ropes were cut and the Lee dashed ahead. The Lee had been running with half the weight of her fuel and was now topped up, with fuel to spare. As the Robert E. Lee passed Memphis, she was a good hour ahead of the Natchez. Thousands of fires could be seen on the shoreline as all of Memphis had stayed up all night to watch the race and cheer.

At Cairo, Cannon and his crew were in full celebration, pouring whiskey to toast an inevitable victory, but they were to suddenly hear the harsh scraping sounds, and feel the tremendous lurching vibrations, of a hull grounding out on a sand bar. The Captain and crew screamed and cursed, and the Robert E. Lee stood motionless. Orders were given to the pilot to turn this way and that, and then reverse in a violent attempt to free the ship. All of a sudden they heard the sound of the keel released from the sand bar, yet no jubilation was felt by the crew of the Lee because, at the same time they heard the steamboat whistle and saw the smoke in the distance as the Natchez, who had made much better time than anyone felt was possible, came into view.

The Robert E. Lee, now at full speed, was neck to neck with the Natchez, and about to enter a narrow channel. Neither boat would give way; they collided heavily, their two sides rubbing together all the way through the channel. Once free, the Natchez pulled ahead, leaving the Lee to follow close behind. At midnight it still seemed like anybody's race but the fog closed in and, with the loss of visibility, came danger. Captain Leathers had the responsibility of passengers, crew, and freight and, for this, he tied up alongside the bank and waited till morning to resume.

Captain Cannon recklessly continued on, wagering all in an attempt to beat the Natchez. His crew tested the river's depth with fathom lines and the Robert E. Lee inched forward, every man aboard praying the boat would not hit a snag or run aground in the night, in the dense fog. After an hour of this slow, tense, groping, the fog broke. The river stood ahead of them, calm and friendly and inviting. The men shouted, and it is said that Captain Cannon turned a complete somersault on deck. He could taste success.

The Robert E. Lee arrived at St. Louis on July 4, three days and eighteen hours after leaving New Orleans. For the winning crew there was a hero's welcome: church bells were ringing, cannons were shot off, locomotive whistles were blowing. Some of the excited mob stormed aboard to greet the captain and crew, almost overturning the boat over by the weight of their numbers.

The Natchez made port six hours and thirty-six minutes later and Leathers and his men were received with equal enthusiasm. Cannon and Leathers were wined and dined in a congratulatory party. Captain Leathers deduced that, after subtracting the six hours' layover, and the time taken by scheduled stops, his actual running time had been faster than Cannon's. Thousands agreed with him, but most bets were paid off on the Robert E. Lee in North America. In Europe they were canceled, since London and Paris felt that the Lee's use of the steamboat "Frank Pargaud", the stripped condition of the boat, and the rejection of freight and passengers, disqualified it as a working steamboat.

Below: The famous Natchez on the left and the Robert E. Lee.

In Canada, the first steam driven paddlewheeler, named the Accommodation, was launched in 1809 in Montreal, Quebec. Other paddlewheel steamboats in Canada include the Frontenac (1816) on Lake Ontario; the General Stacey Smyth (1816) on the Saint John River; the Union (1819) on the lower reaches of the Ottawa River; the Richard Smith (1830) visiting PEI; the Royal William (1831) steaming from Québec to Halifax; and the seagoing Beaver (1836), which first plied the waters off B.C. I have personally been on the Beaver, and can attest that it has been reconditioned and kept up beautifully. The Spitfire (1840) was the first steamboat in St. John's harbour; and the Anson Northup (1859), the first paddlewheeler to cross the international boundary on the Red River. There were twelve paddlewheelers on the Fraser River in British Columbia from 1863 to 1921. Today, a paddlewheeler called the M.V. Native takes folks up and down the Fraser, between the historic towns of New Westminster and Fort Langley, British Colombia.

The Mississippi River was a famous passageway for paddleboats, and the entertainment on board was most commonly provided by jug bands playing the roots of jazz. The experience on board was an entertainment of luxury and splendor. The sound of the paddlewheel and the hissing of steam caused everyone on shore to look up and wave. There was often music, games of chance, dancing, and dinning. It was much more than transportation to many who loved the atmosphere and scenery.

If you go to New Orleans today you can board the Natchez and cruise the Mississippi. I will tell you that, on a beautiful warm day, with a tableful of drinks, it is just a little bit of heaven. It is a must do.

CHAPTER THIRTY SEVEN:
A WOMAN'S STRUGGLE

Life for the North American woman in the 1850s was dismal at best. Women were considered inferior to males and were looked upon as the property of men. The husband was the head of the household and had the final word, sometimes, the *only* word.

Through the mid 1800s, the wife in a middleclass household was considered the child bearer and was not allowed to have a career. Her days were spent embroidering or knitting, while household chores were done by servants. The wife had no legal rights. Property or money that she had when she was single, once married became the possession of the husband. The children were also legally the property of the husband.

A working-class family was a desperately difficult life for the wife. She was expected to bear the children, raise them, and go out to work, usually at a factory, as an agricultural worker, or she could enter domestic service. Families of seven or eight were common. No woman could enter the professions (law or medicine) and they were not allowed to vote in any type of election.

Below: Women struggle for equality.

Below: The organized anti-suffrage movement.

As we entered the Gilded Age (the elegant eighties, gay nineties, and the first decade of the 20th century) not much had changed. Legally, husband and wife were considered one person, and that person was the husband. A married woman could not own property, sign legal documents, or enter into a contract. They could not obtain an education against their husband's wishes, or keep a salary for themselves. If a wife was permitted to work, under the laws, she was required to relinquish her wages to her husband. In certain cases, a woman did not have individual legal liability for her misdeeds, since it was legally assumed that she was acting under the orders of her husband. A husband and wife were not allowed to testify either for, or against, each other.

Below: Suffragist parade in New York City (1917).
The placards displayed more than a million signatures of support.

Single women were not supposed to wear makeup, expose too much flesh, nor go on dates without a chaperone. The restrictions were even tighter in rural areas.

Below: 1913, women demonstrating for the right to vote.

At this point in time, an opportunity to enter into show business was an escape door that offered unforeseen equalities and intellectual opportunities. It came with the additional benefits of receiving admiration from an accepting audience.

The First World War had provided an opportunity for women to work in new jobs, as the men were away, gaining skills they previously hadn't been able to develop. The consumerist nature of the boom also made housework quicker and easier through new inventions like the vacuum cleaner. The contribution they made during the war effort gave the young generation of women the confidence to take charge of their destiny and desires.

The Roaring '20s: In 1920 all women in the United States were granted the vote. In Canada, women in Ontario had been voting since 1884. In 1916 women in Manitoba got the right to vote and the rest of the provinces had everybody voting by 1919, except Quebec, where women were held back until 1940.

**Below: Louise Brooks, actress and dancer,
started the bobbed haircut craze.**

Some of the new age women adopted the nickname of Flapper. This was an age where a woman could go out with a man unaccompanied by a chaperone...and even kiss in the streets! They bobbed their hair and flaunted their disdain for what was, at the time, considered acceptable behavior. Flappers were seen as brash for wearing excessive makeup, drinking, treating sex in a casual manner, smoking, wearing short skirts, driving automobiles, and otherwise flouting social and sexual norms. Flappers were going out - with or without men - and dancing in the jazz halls. It was a much needed, and long awaited, time of rebellion.

Below: Jennifer Nelson dressed to the nines.

By the year 1929, ten million women held jobs. They now had money of their own, and their importance in society was on the increase. Companies had to adjust their advertisements to appeal to women. Movies became focused to the female market. Books were written aimed for the female pocketbook. Henry Ford produced the first Model T automobiles in a choice of colours.

CHAPTER THIRTY EIGHT: SHOE WHEELS

A man had put small wheels under his shoes in 1745 in Europe. However, they were very difficult to make any turns other than wide sweeping ones, and were so hard to steer, and so difficult to stop, they were not at all popular; in fact, they were looked upon as a bit hazardous.

It left a lot of people scratching their heads and pulling their chins. The skating phenomena was stale-mated with little progress being made. Skating proto-types were developed with smaller wooden wheels. The skate had to be strapped to the shoe with a leather thong, and tied. This system was problematic with skates becoming too loose or painfully too tight. With no brakes, stopping was also difficult.

Rubber wheels were introduced in 1852 by the Woodward Skate Company in England. Wheels on skates were made of wood in America up until 1910. Steel wheels were by far the longest lasting and the only real choice for sidewalk enthusiasts.

Below: Wooden roller skates. Circa 1800s

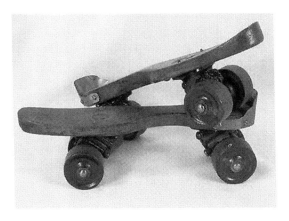

Below: The first in-line skates in 1905

In 1863, the "quad skate", or four-wheel turning roller skate, was first designed in New York City by James Plimpton. By leaning to one side, a pivoting action took place allowing the skate to corner. It was so embraced by the general public, the first indoor skating rinks were opened in 1866, first in New York and then in Rhode Island. The quad skate dominated the marketplace for more than a century. Skating evolved from a pastime to an actual competition sport, with racing, figure skating and speed skating.

- In 1876, William Brown in Birmingham, England patented a design for the wheels of roller-skates. 1876 was to bring us the very important "toe-stop", allowing a braking system.

- In the North America, in the 1880s, mass production had begun and skate sales went through the roof, kicking off one of the largest boom periods for skating.

- In 1884, Levant M. Richardson received a patent for the use of steel ball bearings in skate wheels. This reduced friction, allowing skaters to increase speed with minimum effort. His company in the early part of 1898 began producing skates, mostly for professional racers.

- In the 1890s, a two-piece adjustable roller-skate plate was created that allowed one pair of skates to be worn by people with different show sizes (at different times, of course).

- In 1902, the Coliseum in Chicago opened a public skating rink. Over seven thousand people attended the opening night. Skates usually consisted of a wooden plate that would be strapped onto the shoe or boot with leather straps. The plate had the wheels attached, but there was a consistent problem with the straps slipping or breaking.

- A man named E.H. Barney invented a method of clamping the skate to the shoe or boot by tightening it up with a skate key.

Below: steel roller skates with the skate key
(to be worn on a lanyard around your neck).

- In 1900, the inline skate was patented with two wheels.

- The most popularity that skating would generate was around 1935.

- The Roller Skating Rink Operators Association was developed in the United States in 1937. It is currently named the Roller Skating Association.

- The 1900s saw the first "shoe skates". These were developed for professional skaters. There was also a line of fashionable shoe skates for the wealthy and socially elite. The general public used the clamp-ons.

Below: young skater in 1921.

CHAPTER THIRTY NINE: FLYBOYS AND GIRLS

After WWI pilots returned home to re-enact dogfights at air shows and at fairs. Wing walking was a crowd favorite and the biplane was the choice of many a daredevil when it came to risking their life for money and the admiration of the crowd.

Novelty flying, or stunt flying, became faddish entertainment. Air shows were born, and flying exhibits were welcomed at fairs and festivals. The term "barnstormers" refers to pilots in the 1920s that flew from town to town selling airplane rides. They would commonly get permission to use a farmer's field as a landing strip. However, barnstorming also could mean doing stunt shows in a flying circus, which was the first form of civil aviation.

At this time, there was a surplus of airplanes called the Curtiss JN-4s (referred to as "Jennys"). This was the plane that all the U.S. airmen had operated when learning to fly. The U.S. government decided to sell them off at a fraction of their value. As they originally had cost $5,000. each, they were sold for as little as $200. The airmen who had returned after the war could easily afford to purchase a plane, and they made a living delivering mail, barnstorming, or smuggling, sometimes all three. The lack of federal aviation regulations at the time allowed for outrageously dangerous stunts that produced some fatal outcomes. By 1927, regulations were in place that all but eliminated barnstorming, and the era came to an end.

In 1919, an American navigator and an English pilot completed the first nonstop transatlantic flight.

This was bested when, on May 20th to 23rd, 1927, a 25 year old U.S. airmail pilot named Charles Augustus Lindbergh went from obscurity to instantaneous world fame by making the transatlantic flight solo, with no radio equipment or instruments that might weigh him down. He flew a plane he called "The Spirit of St Louis". The Spirit was a single engine plane with, what he hoped was, enough fuel to get him from New York to Paris. Once in Europe, and unable to tell the direction to Paris, he flew over a fishing boat and, while making a low pass, he turned off his engine and yelled to the fisherman, "Where is Paris?" The fisherman pointed, Lindberg turned the engine back on, and off he went. Lindberg, who was also a U.S. army air force reserve officer, was awarded the nation's highest military declaration, the Medal of Honor, for his bravery and historic achievement.

Below: Charles Lindberg

Amelia Mary Earhart was born on July 24, 1887. She had written bestselling books about flying, and was an inspiration for many women. She was instrumental in forming the Ninety-Nines, which was an organization for female pilots. She was a supporter of the Woman's Equal Rights Movement and the National Woman's Party.

She was flying a twin engine monoplane, which was a Lockheed Model 10E Electra that had been modified with huge fuel tanks for her 29,000 mile round-the-world tour. She was attempting to circumnavigate the globe at its largest circumference. Her only crew member was Fred Noonan, the navigator. This was not intended as a nonstop flight, and the pair departed Miami on June 1, 1937 and, after numerous stops in South America, Africa, the Indian subcontinent, and Southeast Asia, they arrived at Lae, New Guinea on June 29. They had flown 22,000 miles (35,000 km) and most of the journey had been completed. The remaining 7,000 miles (11,000 km) would be over the Pacific Ocean.

They disappeared over the central Pacific Ocean on July 2, 1937. Nothing was ever found of her or her plane.

Below: Amelia Earhart

Notes: 1911 was the year that mail was delivered by plane for the first time. In 1912 the first person to jump from a plane using a parachute, and live to tell about it, was Captain Albert Berry. Although not considered a source of entertainment for some, The Red Baron (WWI German flying ace) was killed by Canadian Ace Roy Brown on April 21, 1918.

**Below: the author's wife; Jennifer Nelson,
in the navigator's seat of a Stearman biplane.**

CHAPTER FORTY: SEABISCUIT

It was following the Great Depression and the nation needed a hero. They needed someone who had been down-and-out to rise up through diversity and, against all odds, become the crowned king, the undefeated champion, the icon of power, the conqueror.

Who would have thought it would be a horse?

The nation had followed his sad story and long lists of defeats, both on and off the track, through bad luck, abuse, self-neglect, and bad temperament. Despite everything that Seabiscuit had working against him, he rose up to become a great champion. Here is his story....

A nation that was struggling in their day-to-day lives to identified with this horse. As for his status, he was considered a true underdog for many years. His body was sort of low-slung and thick, his legs were stubby, and his tail was stunted. He could look clumsy; he was small-framed; his gait was awkward; his foreleg jabbed out wildly when he ran; some referred to the motion as an "eggbeater gait," yet despite all that, and so much more, he was to become the most popular athlete in his time that North America had ever produced.

Now you must understand, Seabiscuit's owners were very disappointed with him. They had spent top dollar on a horse who's sire was Hard Tack, himself the son of Man O` War (both great racing champions) but Seabiscuit developed the worst results in racing history.

As a young horse Seabiscuit showed no interest in running. "He is lazy," according to James Fitzsimmons, Seabiscuit's first trainer. In retrospect, however, it looks like his poor performance was due to the fact that he was pushed too hard. He was forced to run in 43 races when he was three years old. That is more races than most horses run during their entire careers, and in attempt to get him to run as fast as they wanted, they whipped him liberally. Perhaps it was in retaliation, or simply high stress and being demoralized, that Seabiscuit started to refuse his food, and soon weighed some 200 pounds less than he should have. He would also burst out in anger lunging at people, and became known as a mean horse.

Things changed when he was sold to Charles Howard for $8,000., and got a new trainer: Tom Smith. Tom changed Seabiscuit's diet to include high quality Timothy hay and the horse was allowed to sleep in as late as he wanted. Next, Seabiscuit had his stall enlarged to accommodate him and another horse named, Pumpkin, who was very old and quiet. Horses are herd animals and like the company of others. Seabiscuit settled down, became "quite sweet", and was rewarded with a stray dog named Pocatell, and also a spider monkey named Jo-Jo. With all these new entertaining friends sharing his living quarters, Seabiscuit was now happy, and his new, gentler trainer began to work with him.

Below: Seabiscuit in training

His new rider was a Canadian jockey named Red Pollard, and what a surprise they got when Seabiscuit started racing again. Seabiscuit had decided he liked running fast now, and he was winning. They began racing him all up and down the eastern seaboard and he was winning consistently. His past history was common knowledge to race fans, but now all eyes were on Seabiscuit. What seemed like a talentless horse from the beginning of his career, was now a champion. This was an era where folks loved, and needed, a fairy-tale ending.

There was only one horse he had not met on the track and that was the son of Man O` War, his own half-uncle, War Admiral. It was said this horse had inherited Man O` War's tremendous speed. The match race was set for November the 1st, 1938 and so highly publicized that 40 million people tuned in on their radio sets to listen to the outcome. That was one out of every three Americans. Most were rooting for the underdog, Seabiscuit, although the heavy betting was put on War Admiral.

The bell rang, the horses bolted from a walking start. Everyone expected War Admiral to take the lead and hold it, but Seabiscuit bolted full force and stormed into the lead where he stayed right up until they hit the backstretch. Seabiscuit's jockey that day was George Woolf, due to Red Pollard having suffered a knee injury, and George intentionally slowed Seabiscuit down allowing War Admiral to come up nose to nose. Red Pollard had advised George that if he let the other horse give Seabiscuit "the old look in the eye," he'd run twice as fast out of spite. Seabiscuit pulled away from War Admiral and by four lengths, he won the race of the century, lifting a spiritually bankrupt nation from its knees.

Early the following year, to the heartbreak of the American people, Seabiscuit stumbled during a race and ruptured a ligament. He was not expected to ever race again. Seabiscuit went back to California for a nice long rest in attempt to recover. Red Pollard was recuperating here too, and he and Seabiscuit both limped around the property, taking walks together, trying to heal. The nation was saddened with the loss of Seabiscuit who had gotten more press than President Franklin Roosevelt or Nazi leader Adolf Hitler.

But in 1940 the inconceivable took place: Seabiscuit, seven years old, (considered ancient by all standards in racing), the horse that was considered through and written off as a contender, would race in the Santa Anita Handicap for the $121,000.00 purse. This would be his last race and if he won, it would be the greatest come-back in racing history. Early in his career Seabiscuit had run at Santa Anita twice and each time he had lost by a nose. Red Pollard's broken leg was still on the mend, but he intended to ride Seabiscuit despite the chances that his leg could easily re-break during the race.

As they entered the back straight of that big race, Seabiscuit was ready to sprint, but he was boxed in with a horse in front of him on the rail and one ahead to his outside. Suddenly a small gap opened and Pollard yelled,

"Now, Pops!" Seabiscuit burst ahead and was coming into the home stretch. They were all barreling at record speed when Seabiscuit came nose to nose with Kayak II, the lead horse. Red Pollard matched Kayak's gait and waited, his prayers were answered when Kayak made the mistake of giving Seabiscuit "the old look in the eye". In Seabiscuit's mind that took it from a serious race to a personal challenge. Instantly, Seabiscuit shot forward, not just outdistancing the others but constantly gaining speed. One question was on the mind of everyone in attendance, "How is this possible?!" Seabiscuit won the race with the second-fastest time ever run on an American race track for distance to date.

This was his last race. Seabiscuit went home to retire with his old friends Pumpkin, Pocatell, and Jo-Jo.

Below: Seabiscuit and Red Pollard had a special and unique understanding of each other: both had been underdogs in the early years of their lives.

CHAPTER FORTY ONE: PARLOUR TRICKS

Talking to ghosts and spirits was all the rage…

The word "occult" is associated with secret knowledge and practices dealing with the supernatural or "psychic" phenomena, sometimes for the purpose manipulating their clients for financial gain. Some occult practices rely on "demons" or "spirits" to achieve goals, other practitioners claim to be gifted with personal power.

Mediumship is to mediate communication between the deceased and the living through the conduit of spirits. This has been a curiosity dating back to the beginning of time, and in the mid 1800s to the mid 1920s surfaced as a popular social quasi-scientific solution for those who had lost family members or loved ones. This trendy upper-class social gathering proved to be a curiosity to some, an entertainment to others, and a shocking revelation to a few.

Below: A séance in 1930

243

On July 1, 1890 the Ouija board, occasionally referred to as the spirit board or talking board, became available to the public. This was the day it had received a U.S. patent. This system of occult communication had been in existence since 1100 AD in China where it was called Fuji which meant planchette writing. In 1901, the board was officially named the Ouija Board, an ancient Egyptian word meaning "good luck". Real or a toy? The scientific community have been critical, whereas, the mainstream Christian denominations warn that using Ouija Boards can lead to demonic possession. Occultists back it, saying that it truly works, but they stress caution in its use. The Ouija Board was never as popular as it was through the 1920s.

Below: An original Ouija board (1894)

The afterlife is the concept of a realm in which a person's identity or consciousness continues to exist after their body has died, leaving what is thought of as a soul or spirit. The otherworld is often thought of as a spirit world, but this description can become viewed in many different ways when distorted or infused with religious ideals. It is said, and believed by many, that these now dead individuals can develop a line of communication through the help of a medium, shaman, clairvoyant, or psychic (stay with me). In the Victorian era through to the 1920s the paranormal was all the rage. Here is how it started.

The year was 1847. Margaret and Kate Fox, two young girls, had moved with their family into a supposedly haunted house in upstate, New York. They had been living there for three months, all the while hearing a constant borage of unexplainable noises through the night. One evening Margaret and Kate, ages 15 and 11 respectively, were so scared that they spent the night in their parents' bedroom. The noises could be plainly heard by everyone and finally Kate called out, "Mr. Splitfoot, do as I do." She clapped her hands, and heard clapping in reply. Margaret yelled out, "Do as

I do." She clapped four times and was answered with four claps. Their mother Mrs. Fox began to ask a series of questions which could all be answered through varied claps, taps, and stomps, and in doing so they were to realize that they were communicating with the spirit of a man who had been murdered in this same house years before. History shows, some 50 years later a skeleton was found under the house.

The Fox sisters claimed that they had an ability to talk to the dead; overnight they became famous. In 1849, they appeared at Rochester, New York demonstrating their ability to communicate with the dead, and soon were conducting séances for the public. Whether they were frauds or not, it was the Fox sisters that ignited a popular interest in séances and clairvoyants that lasted for over seventy years.

As the profession of mediumship developed, we found two distinct categories: the mental medium, who worked with spoken word or written messages from the spirit world, and the physical medium that had a flare for the dramatic and, therefore, saw a higher profit margin. The physical medium worked with moving tables, blinking lights, tooting horns, and self-extinguishing candles. The greatest effect was the appearance of ectoplasm, a diaphanous matter that was said to be the essence of spirits or ghosts.

Below: Canadian "medium" Mary Marshall. She is demonstrating the appearance of ectoplasm with "spirits" depicted within it. She was later proven as a fraud: the "ectoplasm" was composed of cloth, tissue, and magazine cut-outs of people.

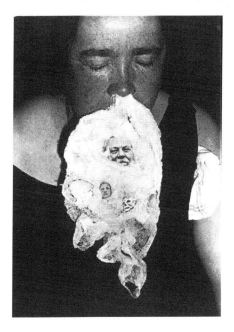

Years later, in 1882, a group of scientists founded the Society for Psychical Research (SPR) in England, and three years later a Harvard psychologist, William James, created the American Society for Psychical Research (ASPR). The two organizations set forth to debunk the charlatans who took peoples' hard-earned money in exchange for what was to become known as parlour tricks. In the 1920s this crusade included the talents of Sir Arthur Conan Doyle (the author of Sherlock Holmes) and Harry Houdini, the famed escapologist and magician.

One of the best known mediums was a woman known as Margery. During her séances, ectoplasm would create phantom limbs on her body. The effect was disturbing and incredibly real looking. She entered a contest conducted by Scientific America, with a grand prize of $2,500. if she could be judged to have the ability to communicate with the dead. During the first presentation she impressed everyone in attendance, even the editor of Scientific American; Malcolm Bird became a true believer and supporter of Margery, and wrote about what he saw in the magazine. Other magazines also ran the story and Houdini's support was implied, which infuriated Harry as he had not been present. After sitting in for a few of Margery's séances, Harry Houdini was able to prove that Margery was, indeed, a fraud. Other examples were exposed again and again and the public finally lost interest in being duped.

CHAPTER FORTY TWO:
HISTORICAL SAYINGS AND FACTS

- The popular Charles "Kid" McCoy boxed his way to success at the end of the 19th century. His technique? To feign illness before bouts, or spread the word to the media that he had neglected his training. Then, when it was fight night, to the surprise of the press and his opponents, McCoy was fit and ready to fight. Reporters kept asking, "Is this the real McCoy?"

- Conestoga wagons had a sealed bottom and sides, so you would float across rivers, creeks, and flooded areas, making it easy for the horses to draw the wagon through water.

- In 1925, the first motel was built in California. It was a motorist hotel (hence the term mo-tel) and featured a two room bungalow, kitchenette, and a private adjoining garage for the car. The cost was $1.25 per night.

- "Sold down the river" entered the American idiom around 1850. It referred to sales of slaves along the Mississippi because, the further south you were sent, the worse the living conditions became.

- The phrase "rule of thumb" is derived from an old English law which stated that you can't beat your wife with a stick that was wider in diametre than your thumb.

- "Got the shaft" refers to the pole that was used to push the bags of decomposed bodies to the rear of a New Orleans funeral crypt.

- "Dead ringer": In some cemeteries, if a comatose victim of premature burial awakened, he would be able to ring a bell to summon help. This is also responsible for the term, "saved by the bell." The person would be seen the next day and people would exclaim, "You look just like the person we buried yesterday!" "Yes, in fact, I am a dead ringer!"

Below: the bell system was to provide a means to call for help in the case of pre-mature in-ground burials.

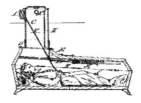

- In the 19th century, upper-class New Orleans buildings had two sets of stairs: one for the ladies and one for the gentlemen. It was so a man would not see a lady's ankles. If he did glimpse them, he was expected to propose marriage.

- In the 19th and 20th centuries, women would fill their wrinkles with wax before applying their makeup. But standing too close to a fireplace could become disastrous, so they would often carry a fan which they held up to block the heat. If someone commented on this, you might hear them reply, "Mind your own bees' wax!"

- Wardrobe cabinets were popular because, in many countries, people were taxed based on the number of rooms in their house, and a closet was considered a room.

- Before the industrial era was a time when workers carried their tools from job to job in a sack. When the job was over, or if the labourer was fired, the boss would hand the worker his tool sack, hence the term "given the sack" or "having been sacked".

- In the frontier days - traveling between homesteads, towns, and small settlements - peddlers and traveling musicians needed to be as silent as possible to avoid bandits and hostile encounters. But, as they approached their destination, they would hang bells around their horse's necks to announce their arrival. That is why we say, "I'll be there with bells on".

- Storekeepers at the general store would sell cloth by the yard, often measured by using his arm as the length of each yard. If the measurement was challenged, two brass tacks were put into the counter, thirty-six inches apart, and the cloth was measured again. This was called "getting down to brass tacks".

- Drunk? Sailing ships are controlled with a system of ropes called halyards, lines, and sheets, and they functioned to move the ship, or hold it in place. The sheets are the ropes controlling the sails. Loosen one and the sails will flap, but two loose will affect the steadiness of the vessel. However, three loose and the ship would go completely off course. From this we got: "Drunk? He's three sheets to the wind!"

- When a salesman is going on and on, and not really telling you what you want to hear, you may say, "Don't give me a song-and-dance". In vaudeville, in order to prepare the scenery for the next big headliner to come on, they would stall by sending out a song-and-dance team who would tell jokes in between songs.

- "Put a sock in it!" means to keep quiet. The old wind-up gramophones had a huge horn where the sound came out, but they were not electronic, so there was no volume control. The best way to quiet it down was to shove a sock in the throat of the horn.

- In the 1930s, being questioned by the police was sometimes called "getting the third degree". This came from the Masonic Lodge and refers to the three degrees of membership. Degree one: entered apprentice; Degree two: Fellowship; but Master Mason was the most difficult to pass, and it was the third degree.

- "Dressing to the nines": This term originated in England, but became a common phrase in North America. In the theatre, the furthest seats from the stage cost one pence, and the closest cost nine pence. So sitting in these expensive seats meant dressing up so you would fit in with the wealthy. You were "dressing to the nines".

- Many of the wealthiest ladies would attend social functions carrying their tiny lap dogs with them. Dressing up was sometimes referred to as "putting on the dog".

NOTES LEFT FOR YOU TO FIND:

I suggest reading:

Mack Sennett's book called "The King of Comedy".

"Very Special People" by Frederick Drimmer . It is about the story of the Freak Show.

To widen your horizons further, I fully endorse the writings of an acquaintance, and possibly one of the most knowledgeable historians living today: Mr. Trav S.D. Look for one of his books entitled "Chain of Fools". He has another book that is fantastic, and is a must read, entitled "No Applause- Just Throw Money".

"Bix – Man and Legend" by Richard M. Sudhalter, Philip R. Evans, and William Dean Myatt, is excellent.

If you would like the life story of Stephen Foster, I recommend: "Doo-Dah!" by Ken Emerson.

"Keaton" by Rudi Blesh, is the ultimate Buster Keaton book. Please read it. It is very good.

"With a Banjo on My Knee" by Dr. Rex Ellis, is a book about slavery, the banjo, and the journey they took together.

"Such Melodious Racket" by Mark Miller: this is about the lost history of jazz in Canada.

"The Fabulous Kelly - King of the Medicine Show" by Gordon Sinclair, offers real insight to the medicine show world.

"The Comedy World of Stan Laurel" by John McCabe

"Harpo Speaks" by Harpo Marx. This is everything you would have hoped for.

"Gracie – A Love Story" by George Burns. This is one of my all-time favourite books. It walks you through the years of vaudeville with laughter, a brave heart, and tears. Give this to someone you love (after you have read it).

"Tommy and Jimmy: the Dorsey Years" by Herb Sanford

"Reminiscing With Sissle and Blake" by Robert Kimball and William Bolcom.

WELL, THIS IS IT, THE END OF THE BOOK.
AS LADY GODIVA SAID,
"I NOW COME TO MY CLOTHES".

ABOUT THE AUTHOR

Douglas Edward Fraser is a showman, musicologist, vocalist, and performer on tenor guitar, banjo and is a concert kazooist. Douglas hails from three generations of professional entertainers, and has been on stage since the age of three. Douglas's father was a Ringling Brothers Circus star performer, vaudevillian with partner Amos Jacobs (later to be Danny Thomas), a stand-up comic, and matinee crooner. His mother performed on the Shubert Circuit in vaudeville, and his grandmother toured with Buffalo Bill's Wild West Show.

Douglas was part of the jug band resurgence in the 1960's and has played jazz in concert coast to coast. He has been in television, movies, and radio shows throughout the years.

Douglas worked as an opening act for such greats as Buddy Rich, Les Brown and his band of Renown, and Stan Getz. Throughout his career, Douglas had in-depth conversations with musical legends such as Eubie Blake, Earl Hines, Hezzie (Hoosier Hot Shots), and Mousie Garner (Spike Jones & the City Slickers, one of the original Three Stooges, and vaudeville partner to Red Skelton). These personal opportunities for Douglas were like opening an encyclopedia to the past.

Professor Fraser takes history on stage with him, and audiences thank him for it.

www.thegenuinejugband.com

*Douglas Edward Fraser has also written "The Prepper's Book of Ideas" available at Amazon in paperback form and as a Kindle ebook.